LEGACY OF THE INDUS

پاکستان

LEGACY OF THE INDUS

A Discovery of Pakistan

by

Samina Quraeshi

New York · WEATHERHILL · Tokyo

All quoted material in the book, with the exceptions of the poems, written in English, by Salman Tarik Kureshi and that from English-language sources, was translated by the author.

Romanization of foreign words: Familiar spellings found in Western dictionaries and atlases are used for some words and most geographical names; otherwise, terms are given in the author's own transliteration.

The photographs facing chapter-opening pages (pages 24, 56, 104, and 148) show embroidery patterns, one of the traditional folk crafts of Pakistan. In keeping with Islamic law, the patterns are geometric or floral and nonrepresentational, but they display an intricacy and richness that belies any limits on the imagination. The motifs, of course, vary from tribe to tribe and from village to village.

The calligraphy on the title page is the word Pakistan *in Urdu script.*

First edition, 1974

Published by John Weatherhill, Inc., 149 Madison Avenue, New York, N.Y. 10016, with editorial offices at 7-6-13 Roppongi, Minato-ku, Tokyo. Copyright © 1974 by Samina Quraeshi; all rights reserved. Poems on pp. 8, 76–77, 91–92, 96, 132, 133, 137, 190–91, and 212–14 copyright © 1974 by Salman Tarik Kureshi. Printed in Japan.

LCC 73-88465   ISBN 0-8348-0093-4

Contents

In memory of my father
Sheikh Abdus Sattar Quraeshi
one of the many men
who dreamed this country
and made it happen

Such plastic-clear perspectives stun the senses:
Eagle-shunned crags at wing-tip height,
flashing like solar mirrors on the mountains.

Boulders caressed to silt by water . . .
deep, round valleys, robed in cloud
against the crag-carving sunlight on the peaks.

Look down! Look down!
There, a three-minute drop beneath,
the hunching bases of mountains nestle into—
no, not the plains—the clouds.

White river, turning brown at mouths of valleys . . .
brown river, brown as people . . .
square fields and endless flatness of the plains.

And centuries of cloud have melted, valleys
have sweated froth-white cascades
to draw that long, brown line down to the sea.

SALMAN TARIK KURESHI

Photographs, pages 9–17.

1. *The Indus flows from the perpetual snow and glaciers of the Karakoram range into Gilgit. The pasture- and orchard-bordered cascades leap with trout in these far northern reaches of Pakistan.*

2. *High pine forests and terraced fields frame the waters of the Indus as they flow down from Balakot to Babusar in the Kagan valley.*

3. *The silver Indus in the Swat valley, before it meanders onto the plains.*

4. *The Indus nurtures and nourishes the villages that teem along its banks, shaping patterns of living according to its moods.*

5. *Near Karachi, the swollen Indus slips quietly into the ocean.*

Preface

This book is an examination of the people who live in the regions drained by the Indus River. The country they inhabit, the country called Pakistan, was born on the fourteenth of August 1947, when the tides of empire receded from the shore of their river. Though their country is young, its borders circle one of the most ancient corners of the human world. The long brown waters of the Indus flow through fifty-five centuries of civilization. History is an integral part of life here, as often in its denial as in its enrichments, and inevitably history is a major theme of this book.

History has shaped the lives and thought processes of the Indus basin's sixty million people; it has entered in unexpected ways into the ordinary routines of living. The pageant of many races, many civilizations, many cultures has merged to form the unique soul of this land. But the reader of this book will not, I hope, come to it as a historical text; it is not meant to be an accurate, chronological narrative. It is a personal view of history, frequently of its interesting corners and little bylanes—the personal view of an involved observer of present-day life in the Indus Valley.

The four provinces of Pakistan that lie along the Indus and its tributaries present many contradictions, many anomalies. Theirs is an unusual society: It juxtaposes heart-stopping beauty with shabby deprivation, fecundity with desolation, conservatism with exuberance—and makes of them a complex single entity, impossible to summarize in any generalization.

It can arouse extreme emotions; involvement and value judgments are continually demanded. But value judgments require agreement on standards and criteria, while here the varieties of experience and consciousness are too many and too varied. They often pull in opposite directions; one cannot be neutral. Fascination does not cancel an equally intense revulsion; it can form a bewildering whole with it. And there are many different fascinations and revulsions operating on the consciousness of an involved observer of this land. The complex, many-sided whole is infinitely more than the sum of its parts.

The Indus regions of Pakistan make up a land of varied hues and textures. There are those that glow deeply in twilight colors, and those that parade in peacock-proud extravagance. There are bright hues and pale hues and the ever-present flat brown of the earth. There are textures that are silken and others that evoke a strange, dusty poignancy. There is also much that is abrasive or harsh,

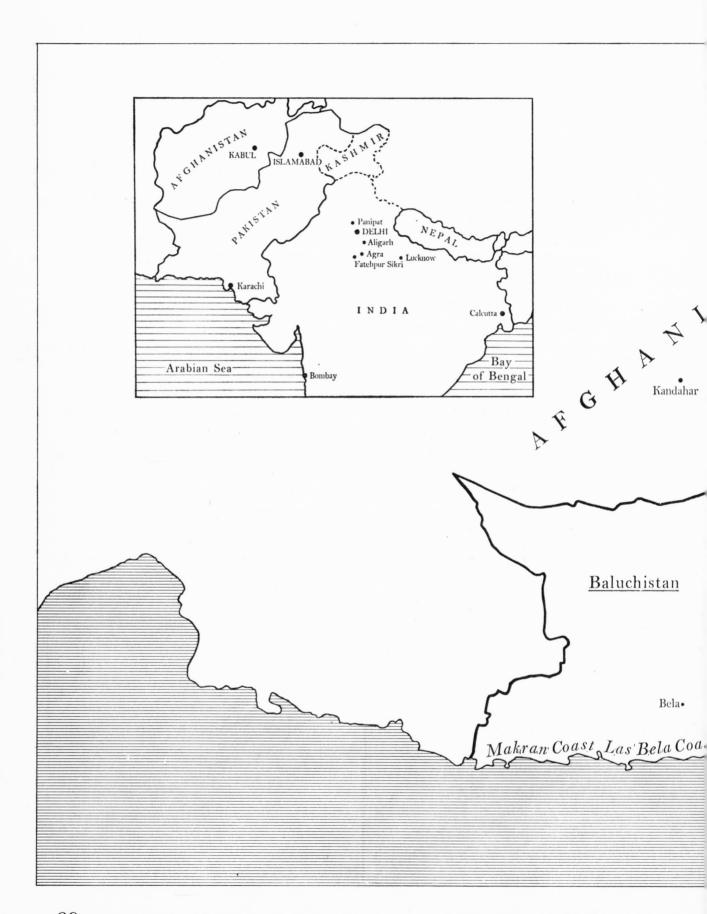

shabby or meretricious, and all that is stagnant and decaying; much that is sensuous and strong, and much that is germinal.

In this book, I have tried to express something of these many textures. I have tried to invoke the incredible complexity and capture it in a single volume.

Geography, sociology, ethnography, language, religion—each discipline is a different approach to this country and its people. These are woven, with history and pictures and words and the stories of people, into a long, close look at a land. If this look seems sometimes too selective, the emphases too personal, it is because I make no pretensions to either great erudition or scholarly objectivity. I wish to evoke, not to analyze.

The questions posed here are deceptively simple: What does it feel like to be a Pakistani? What is the flavor, texture, smell of this country? The reader will find words and pictures laid out in many juxtapositions for him to look at, dip into, savor, consider—and form his own impression of the original.

The core of this book is the ancient heart of Pakistan, its villages and the people who live in them. It is a small celebration of Pakistani village life. And it is one woman's attempt at describing her land and its many-hued people.

S.Q.

LEGACY OF THE INDUS

1 The Indus Valley in History

The South Asian subcontinent is separated from the rest of Asia by a wall of mountain ranges—the Hindu Kush, the Sulaiman, the Karakoram, and the Himalayas. Below these are the seemingly endless plains drained by the Indus, the Ganges, and the Brahmaputra rivers. In the geological youth of the world, the entire subcontinent was part of the ocean bed. Its ring of mountains was a wall of cliff-shored islands holding back the waves from the Asian heartland as they now hold back the monsoon clouds. The ocean receded; the sea bed became fertile plains. Rivers began to find their way to the now distant ocean. The longest of the three great subcontinental rivers is the Indus, in Pakistan. The river has given its name to a country and a religion—ironically, not the country through which it flows nor the religion of the people who live by its waters. It is fed by many streams from the mountains of Tibet, the Soviet Union, and Afghanistan. Five other major rivers flow into the Indus: the Jhelum, Chenab, Ravi, Sutlej, and Beas.

This book is about the people who live along these waters and the people who live in the deserts deprived of these waters. They speak many languages—Urdu, Punjabi, Sindhi, Pashto, Baluchi, Brahui, Gujarati, to name some—reflecting the diversity of their historical and cultural experience. The people of the Indus live in four provinces of Pakistan:

The North West Frontier Province (or NWFP) in the rugged lower reaches of the Hindu Kush and Himalaya mountains, with a population of 11 million and its capital at fabled Peshawar.

Punjab (the name means "five waters"), stretching across the five eastern tributaries of the Indus from the Himalayan foothills to the tip of the southern desert, with a population of 32 million and its capital at Lahore.

Baluchistan, in the rocky plateaus and hills that comprise the west of this land; just over 2 million people live in this province, whose capital is at Quetta.

Sind, in the plains of the south, with its incredible wealth of history, its 14 million people, and its provincial capital of Karachi.

They are the products of unnumbered historical permutations and combinations, the fusions and clashes of fifty-five centuries of civilization.

THE CONQUERORS

In the 1920s an expedition of the India Archeological Survey under Sir John Marshall excavated an interesting mound of earth in the Sind region of then British India. This particular earthy protuberance was called Moenjodaro by the locals—"the place of the dead." Sir John and his party discovered one of the world's most ancient cities beneath it. Up to that time the ancient settled areas along the Tigris-Euphrates and the Nile river systems had seemed to merit the title of cradle of civilization; now the Indus was making its claim, and new theories had to be devised. Other sites were investigated, and the cities of the Indus

Valley were unearthed—Harappa, Chanhu-daro, Lothal, Kot Diji—highly developed cities that told of a civilization which had begun around 3000 B.C., reached its apex by 2000, and completely perished by 1000 B.C.

The Indus Valley (or Harappan) civilization extended over an area very much larger than either ancient Egypt or Sumer. There are traceable connections between these three most ancient of civilizations: Correspondences in pottery decoration and design, beads from Egypt in the remains of Harappa tell of commerce during the remotest centuries of time. Perhaps caravans, perhaps ships, passed between these racially distinct civilizations—Hamitic Egypt, Semitic Sumer, and Dravidian Harappa. At first it was believed that the Harappan people were Semitic—an offshoot of the Sumerians. But further evidence, including the physiognomy of their statues, suggests they were a Dravidian people similar to the present inhabitants of South India, the Tamils of Ceylon, and the Brahuis of Baluchistan; that they were, in fact, the "black savages" written of in the Hindu mythology of the later Aryans.

"Savages" they certainly were not. By all available evidence, they were a gentle and gracious people. Their cities were designed with wide streets, rectangular blocks, and efficient drainage systems in accordance with a well-organized plan. In fact, evidence from the ruins suggests a degree of control and planning under a central civic authority unknown to other early civilizations. Theirs was a well-ordered society whose people could afford many of the amenities of life: substantial houses (many with bathrooms), graceful pottery, tools of copper and bronze. In and around the cities, the intermittent floods of the Indus left silt deposits that gradually raised the ground level. Builders then erected new structures and additions on the foundations of the old. The wealthier citizens lived in substantial brick houses, the poorer people in small brick cottages.

Little is known of their religion, which seems to have centered around a cult of the mother goddess. It may have included worship of the fanciful animals found depicted on the celebrated Harappan seals; on the other hand, these seals may have had only secular significance. It certainly included strands that have passed into Hinduism, as have many of its gods. Their system of government seems to have been one of autonomous city-states (not unlike those of Sumer) with common standards and customs. But the degree of cultural correspondence among the various cities suggests some "federal" authority, and good communications.

A static quality seems to have pervaded the Harappan civilization. Over the twenty centuries of their existence, the towns and cities seem to have changed only in that they grew in size and were periodically raised higher to avoid floods. The process of decline, for which there were many causes, was complete by about 1000 B.C. Stagnation and internal population pressures, the felling of forests and consequent climatic and ecological changes, plagues, famines, and the constantly changing course of the Indus River—each contributed to the demise of one or the other city. The last of the Harappan cities and villages were destroyed by invaders.

The Dravidians (more correctly the Dravida) had themselves once been invaders. There are a few half-savage tribes in the jungles of central India who are believed to be the aboriginal inhabitants of the subcontinent. The Dravidians, who came from somewhere else, in the time before history was conceived, appear to have subjugated and exterminated the ancestors of these savages before building the cities of the Indus Valley and themselves being subjugated by the white invaders from the north and west.

It seems that, about every five centuries, conquering nomads from Central Asia have entered the Indus Valley. The Aryans came in two main waves—the first around 1500 B.C. and the second, around 1000 B.C. The Persian emperor Darius (on whose gravestone is inscribed "a Persian, son of a Persian, an Aryan of Aryan descent") annexed the Indus regions and opened them to Scythian settlers in the fifth and fourth centuries B.C. White Huns (Ephthalites) entered this region in the first century B.C. and again in A.D. 500 (the Scythians and White Huns were absorbed into the "Aryan" communities). The Muslim Afghans and Moghuls, who conquered the upper reaches of the Indus region in the twelfth and sixteenth centuries, respectively, also came from Central Asia. But we are running ahead of this historical narrative. We were talking of the early Aryan invasions.

Nomadic tribesmen left their homes in the Caucasus and began entering the subcontinent about 1500 B.C., shortly after similar hordes had entered Persia, Turkey, and Greece and shortly before they began to populate Europe. In Indian and Persian mythology, these people are known as the "Arya" or "Aryans." The term is loose and inaccurate and is used to describe Caucasian peoples of many different origins. Their descendants are the present-day inhabitants of Europe,

Pakistan, northern India, Iran, Turkey, and North America. Their languages are the basis for what is now called the Indo-European group of languages. In the Indus Valley, the Aryans pressed steadily southward and overpowered and destroyed the Harappan cities. Settling in these regions, they founded the Hindu civilization and religion. And they integrated the remaining Dravidians and the children of varying degrees of miscegenation into a new social order—the caste system, the first coherent system of apartheid in human history.

Caste determines each Hindu's profession and place in society from his birth to his death. The "twice-born" Aryan belonged to either the Brahmin or Kshatriya castes (priests, teachers, lawyers, doctors in the first case; rulers, chieftains, soldiers, and administrators in the second). The but "once-born" Aryans—a euphemism for those of mixed Aryan and Dravidian blood—were consigned to the Vaisya castes: farmers, traders, herdsmen, craftsmen, workers, and domestic servants. There were also the casteless—the "untouchables"—who cremated the Aryan dead, swept Aryan floors, and disposed of excrement. They were the children of the dark-skinned Dravidians, and the touch of even their shadows could defile the karma of the twice-born.

The main body of the original Aryan invaders settled across northern India to the east of the Indus Valley. Other Caucasian tribes—Persians, Scythians, White Huns—entered the subcontinent in their wake. They too were welcomed as "Aryans" and settled in what is now Pakistan.

The Hindu civilization and its Buddhist offshoot (later reabsorbed into Hinduism) were disturbed by a Greek invasion in the fourth century B.C. Alexander and his men poured through the northern mountain passes. Meeting little resistance from the scattered clans they first encountered, they fought no major battle until they neared what is now the city of Jhelum in northern Punjab, on the banks of the river of that name. An Aryan king named Raja Pora (recorded as Porus by the Greeks) ruled that part of the Punjab plain. He had tried to negotiate a treaty with the Greeks, granting them safe passage through his territories on condition that they respect the lives and property of his subjects. Learning that his emissary to Alexander had failed to conclude the treaty—had in fact been beheaded by the pupil of Aristotle—Pora rode out to meet the invaders.

His men were daunted by the reputation for savagery that had preceded the actual arrival of the Greeks. To rally their morale, Pora rode to battle at their head. It was a foolhardy gesture, and a futile one. He was wounded at the onset and fell from his horse. His men, believing their king to be dead, broke formation and were completely routed by the Greeks.

Alexander chivalrously restored the injured Pora to his domain—as a viceroy—and pressed on southward. Most Aryan chieftains were ineffective in battle against him; others capitulated. Alexander and his men marched down the length of the Indus and eventually left the subcontinent, some sailing from the Sind coast and some marching across Baluchistan and into Persia.

Although the Greeks made little impression on India, contact with the Hellenic civilization in the northwest of the subcontinent, particularly in the kingdom of Gandhara, continued long after the invaders had left. Gandhara covered the better part of present-day Afghanistan, the NWFP, and the northern regions of the Punjab; it contained great cities—Pushkalavati (Peshawar) and Takshashila (Taxila)—and the art of the Greco-Buddhist culture that flourished there in the first few centuries of the Christian era bears ample witness to the richness of this synthesis.

The other Greek legacy in the subcontinent is found in the names by which a river, a country, and a religion are known to the world. The river along which Alexander campaigned was known to the natives as the Sind (it still is). Alexander recorded it as the Sinthos, and subsequent Roman historians and cartographers as the Sindhus. The lands he invaded were the "Lands of the Sinthos," and the people were the "Sinthoos." Over the years, the Sinthos-Sindhus became the Indus and its people, the Indoos or Hindoos. Later Arab traders called the subcontinent "Hindoostan" (Land of the Hindoos), and sometimes "Hindia." The latter name underwent a European corruption to "India," and the term Hindoo began to be used for the religion rather than the region. In fact, the Hindus had no name of their own for their religion, and the land was known by the separate names of the various kingdoms it accommodated. Had the Hindus chosen a name for their faith, they would more likely have called it after the Ganges or the Brahmaputra—the two rivers sacred to their creed—than the Indus.

In Hindu mythology Raja Indra, King of Creation, plays with visions of cosmic cycles—eons following one another in the endlessness of time, eons contemporaneous in the infinities of space, but all working into endlessly recurring and incomprehensible patterns. The metaphor is not inapt for the successive civilizations that have passed like incidents in the life of the Indus Valley. They have followed many patterns, each unique but with odd similarities to the preceding one. Before its disappearance, each has left something to be absorbed by its successor.

According to Hindu sages, the universe evolves in eons-long world cycles, which are dreams dreamed by Brahma, the all-spirit, the calyx of the lotus that grows from Lord Vishnu's navel. Each world cycle is made up of four *yugas*, or ages of the world: *krita, treta, dvapara*, and *kali*—the four throws of the Indian dice game. Krita yuga, the first of the ages, is the perfect or "four-quartered" age. *Dharma*, the moral order of everything, is stable on its four legs, like a cow. Men and women are virtuous and devote their lives to their ordained karma; Brahmins are saintly, rulers just and chivalrous, and the lower castes fruitful and suitably obedient. As the life processes of the world organism gain momentum, moral order loses ground. Dharma disappears, quarter by quarter, to be replaced by its converse. The treta yuga is the "three-quartered" age. The modes of life of the castes have become less than perfect; duties have to be learned and are no longer spontaneous laws of human action. The dvapara yuga is the age of dangerous balance between imperfection and perfection, dark and light. The cow of ethical order, instead of standing firmly on four legs, balances precariously on two. Men become subject to desires and eager for earthly possessions; they become ambitious and acquisitive and disobedient to their karma.

This process heralds the dark birth of the kali yuga—the black age. The Vishnu Purana, an ancient religious treatise, says this is the age "when property confers rank, wealth buys virtue, passion is the sole bond of union between husband and wife, falsehood the source of success, sex the only means of enjoyment, and ceremonial trappings are confused with religion." In short, this is the present age. This kali yuga began, according to some computations, on Friday, February 18, 3102 B.C. It will last for almost another 427,000 years, after which the perfect krita yuga will dawn again. Order and beauty will have been regained by the fulfillment of karma.

The heyday of Hindu rule in the Indus Valley (the "golden era" of the Gupta kings, from the fourth to the sixth centuries) is regarded by Hindus as a relatively luminous patch in this kali yuga. Much of northern India achieved a loose imperial unification. Hindu princes ruled in the Indus regions more or less continuously from the time the land pulled itself together from Alexander's depredations to the time the Muslim incursions began—a period of about fourteen hundred years, interrupted in the fifth century by the invasion of the White Huns, who settled in the plains and intermarried with the Aryans. The White Huns were a different people from the Huns who pillaged the early kingdoms of Europe. They were a Caucasian (not Mongoloid) people, whose origins are obscure. The word *Hun* is derived from the Sanskrit *Hoona*, which was a generic term for all foreigners.

The gentle faith preached by the former prince Siddhartha, who changed his name to Gautama and became known to future generations as Buddha, had appeared among many Aryans prior to the Greek invasion. An organic offshoot of the Hindu religion, it was initially only a particular school of Hindu thought, but it threatened the premises of the older creed in many important ways. Buddhism spread throughout the Gandhara kingdom in the north and the regions of Sind in the south. It also won many converts in what is now Punjab. The ruling castes at first tolerated this faith, but later it was actively propagated in many parts of the subcontinent by members of noble families who had themselves become Buddhist (including a few emperors). Eventually, however, there was a Hindu resurgence. Brahmin priests, while acknowledging the long-dead Gautama as an avatar, an incarnation of the supreme god Vishnu, proceeded to persecute his followers. Many Buddhists were welcomed back to Hinduism, reabsorbed into the mother body; others were suppressed and exterminated in a series of systematic purges lasting well over a century. Today there are very few Buddhists in the land of Siddhartha's birth.

One of the reasons for the particular appeal of Buddhism in the Indus regions was its rejection of the caste principle. The early Aryan settlers had tended to move eastward into the plains of the Ganges. The later Aryans and the other Caucasian people who had followed them into the subcontinent proved a little awkward to fit into the caste system evolved by their predecessors. Their place among the ranks of the twice-born was definitely merited (no possibility of Dravidian intermixture), but it would challenge or disturb already existing priorities and precedents. Grudgingly, caste status was conferred on a case by case basis to the clans of the newcomers. The phenomenon was inevitably a disquieting one for such a closed order, and resentments and suspicions existed on both sides. The castelessness of Buddhism found these "new" Aryans receptive. It was in the lands of the Indus, where these clans had principally settled, that Buddhism found its readiest converts, as did later Islam. These regions were an area of great ethnic mobility throughout the Hindu period; migration of populations into and out of the Indus Valley was a characteristic of the times.

Before the coming of the Aryans, the Dravidians in the Indus Valley had evolved from a Neolithic farming people to an urbanized folk living in cities surrounded by supporting villages. The Aryans, although they destroyed most of these settlements when they entered the region, adopted the principles of a settled civic order (along with many religious and cultural modes) from their racial predecessors and transformed themselves from nomadic herdsmen into farmers. They in turn built their own cities, but farming remained the basis of economic life and the village, the unit of society.

The central role of the village in Indian society was established during the Hindu period. In due course, a complex bureaucratic system developed on this base; it reached its peak during the reign of the Muslim kings. The ancient Hindu village, however, was not merely a small town; it was a unit in itself, organized as a self-governing commune. The lands surrounding each village were cultivated as a collective by the farming castes living there. Weavers, potters, cobblers, smiths, carpenters and other craftsmen, traders and bankers, priests, judges, and recordkeepers—all were also maintained by the commune-village. Their services to the community were rewarded with a regular stipend from the produce of the village. The job of rulers and princes was one of arbitrating claims between different villages; guaranteeing the security of the villages in their domain (as much against their own soldiers as against outside invaders); providing for public works like canals, roads, and bridges; and maintaining a police force to guard the roads between villages. Princes, their soldiers and courtiers, the various government functionaries, the merchants, traders, and artisans who catered to their needs—these were the citizens of the towns.

There was no significant hereditary landowning class of the European or Japanese type. Between the ruler (whether a local chieftain, petty prince, king, or emperor) and his subjects was the Indian equivalent of a civil service, the bureaucratic nobility. There were government functionaries who collected taxes from the villagers and executed the monarch's commands. They did not hold office by right of birth, nor necessarily for a lifetime. They were governors and tax collectors who, though wreathed in grandiloquent titles, were appointed from time to time by the court. Like civil servants in all ages, they could be posted to any part of the kingdom they served at any time. Any property they acquired was forfeit to the crown after death; they were not allowed any heirs. Although the share of collected taxes that constituted their stipends gave them a great deal of discretionary wealth, it had therefore to be spent in their lifetimes. And it was, on the legendary opulence and luxury of the Indian nobility. They kept elephants and built pleasure houses, bought exquisite silks, and were patrons of the arts.

The Maurya kings began codifying this system in the last few centuries B.C. as a means of systematizing the tribute from their dependencies. It was given its final shape by the Moghuls, and it lasted until the end of the eighteenth century, when the British awarded title deeds to nobles they favored. With the Permanent Settlement of 1793, under which title deeds to land were first introduced, the whole concept of property ownership in the subcontinent was transformed. In the Indus regions, the system of the Mauryas found firm roots in Punjab and the Peshawar valley. In the regions of Sind and Baluchistan, where relatively distant courts could not easily exercise control, local chieftains appointed to office tended to pass their offices on to their sons. Thus, the semblance of a hereditary system, albeit one based on inheritance of power and not property, did develop in the southern reaches of the Indus, as well as in some other parts of the subcontinent. The tribes of the northwestern mountains remained unaffected by the governmental systems of the plains throughout most of history. What protection or public works could an outside ruler provide these self-sufficient people in their mountain fastnesses? And who dared to collect taxes?

Like many other institutions in this part of the world, the system had an inbuilt tendency to stasis. Society was disparate, fragmented. There was little contact between town and country; there was no organic relationship between ruler and subjects. The system itself was stable. It survived, with various modifications, from the second to the nineteenth centuries; but the people at the top had a high turnover rate—kings and dynasties came and went. The lack of any strong ties between ruler and ruled made it that much easier for the former to be deposed without significant opposition from the people.

This "perfect" system, based as it was on a stable "four-quartered" social structure of hereditary castes (even among the later Muslims, converts tended to follow the traditional occupations of their former castes), demonstrated its flaws as it developed. Perhaps it may be said to have been in its krita stage during the time of its nascence in the Maurya period. As it developed and stabilized, various social processes gained momentum: for one thing, no barons meant no Magna Carta; no inheritance meant no accumulation of potentially productive capital. It may be said to have entered a treta stage about the time of the Muslim conquests. The dvapara stage of Indian society was the time of its complete development under the Moghuls, when its faults had become most evident. And the kali yuga of the subcontinental social system occurred during the bloody years of Moghul imperial decline and disintegration; in this age, the British arrived as traders and stayed to change the maps and the basis of society.

ISLAM IN THE INDUS VALLEY

The religion of the Mussulmans was first propagated in the Arabian cities of Medina and Mecca. It was a religion within the monotheistic tradition of the other great Semitic faiths, Judaism and Christianity. It posited one God, whose Final Messenger is the Prophet Mohammed, and a Day of Judgment leading to an afterlife in Heaven or in Hell. It outlined an unusually detailed system of ethical conduct. Its holy book is the Koran, which is believed to have been revealed by God to Mohammed in its entirety. The followers of this faith are called Mussulmans or Muslims.

Islam spread with phenomenal rapidity among the Arabs, who were at the same time becoming a single political unit. For the first time, these desert tribes, with their traditions of oratory and sonorous poetry, became a single nation. Within a very few years their new religion was being carried to other peoples and places, most notably to the Persians. The Arab nation, new as it was, came spilling out of its borders to become an Arab empire that at its height covered Spain; North Africa; much of West and East Africa; the entire Middle East; parts of Eastern Europe; parts of Mongolia; the whole of Turkey, Persia, and Central Asia; and part of the South Asian subcontinent. There were also important outposts in Malaya (modern Malaysia) and the East Indies.

There was a startling intellectual efflorescence in this empire, a historically unique blossoming of the arts and sciences. Proselytizing faiths are not generally known for tolerance of the cultural and intellectual institutions of others, and the accumulated knowledge of centuries is often destroyed—or branded heretical—by religious zealots. The Arabs were an exception in this regard. They burned no books; in fact, they preserved much that the world might have lost, such as the writings of Plato and Aristotle. Absorbing the knowledge and philosophies of the cultures they encountered, they emerged with rich new syntheses. But their empire was a relatively short-lived structure. Empires, it seems, require monarchs and strong centralized control. The elective caliphate and the loosely democratic traditions of Bedouin tribal society were inadequate for imperial needs. The Islamic faith, however, survived wherever they had ruled (except in Spain). By their own avowal, the Arabs had set out to carry the message of Islam to the world, and in this they had succeeded; over a fifth of the world's people today are Muslim.

In the seventh and eighth centuries, as the new empire formed and expanded, Islam came to the Indus Valley. It came in two different ways: as the creed of conquering invaders, and as the preaching of certain very holy men. The invaders arrived by land through the mountain passes in the north, and by sea in the south. In 664, an Arab army came through the Khyber Pass and marched down the Punjab plains. The Arabs penetrated as far as Multan in south Punjab before they were thrown back and expelled. About the same time, several survey and trading expeditions landed on the coast of Sind, whose population was then predominantly Buddhist and whose Hindu rulers had embarked on an anti-Buddhist campaign to expel this casteless heresy from their lands. The Arab expeditions were therefore welcomed enthusiastically by the people. The religious head of Sehwan, for example, called on his fellow Buddhists to seek Arab support against the Hindus. When the soldiers and ships of Mohammed bin Qasim—an Arab admiral—landed in Sind in the early eighth century, local Buddhists assisted them in seizing the province. At the end of a successful two-year campaign, Qasim set up a vice-regency of the Umayyad caliphate in Sind, which he and his successors ruled for fifty years. After that period Sind (to which the province of Multan had subsequently been added) became a kingdom in its own right, ruled by princes of mixed Arab and local pedigree. The capital of this kingdom was at Thatta.

In the eleventh century, an army of Turks from what is now Afganistan under Sultan Mahmood of Ghazni entered the subcontinent through the Khyber Pass. What had begun as pillaging forays turned into a protracted series of nearly annual engagements between Mahmood's forces and those of the Rajput chieftains who were at that time asserting their supremacy in the Punjab and other parts of northern India. But Mahmood's raids were without permanent effect; it was not until the end of the twelfth century that firm foundations were laid for the Muslim domination of northern India by Mohammed of Ghauri. In 1192 Mohammed, after a series of campaigns, finally triumphed over the near-legendary chieftain of the Chauhan clan, Prithviraj. Mohammed and his men occupied the Peshawar valley, the Punjab, and many regions well to the east of Delhi. In the south they reached Multan; finding their Arab coreligionists already in power there, they concluded pacts and withdrew from those reaches.

The riverine plains of the Punjab promised Mohammed and those who followed him a degree of ease and wealth undreamed of in the stern mountains of their homeland. There seemed little point in returning with the trophies of temporary plunder after the series of wars they had fought, and anyhow this land was pleasant. Mohammed of Ghauri, conqueror of Ghazni, became as well conqueror of Hindustan. Under his generals, one of whom had formerly been his slave, a kingdom of considerable size and power was established. Mohammed himself was killed in 1206 on his way to Ghazni, but in the same year his "slave" general, Qutb-ud-din, became the first sultan of Delhi. Qutb-ud-din was by all accounts a stern man, but a just and not unenlightened ruler. Under his successors and the many dynasties of Afghan monarchs that followed them, the Delhi sultanate extended itself over the whole of northern India except for Sind-Baluchistan.

In the context of the early Muslim invaders and the Delhi sultanate, the label "Afghan" is only a convenient term of reference. There was no Afghan nationality as such, and the present state of Afghanistan was not founded until the eighteenth century. The first "Afghans" who invaded India were Turks, who were followed by various Persian- and Pashto-speaking ethnic groups from the city-states of what is now the territory of Afghanistan. With Muslim kingdoms firmly established, many Muslim nationalities entered the Indus Valley. In fact, such migrations and the arrival of wandering holy men had begun in trickles well prior to the Afghan military invasions. Persians came, and Tajiks from Central Asia; Urghuns and Tarkhans made their long trek from the Caucasus and eventually took Sind from the partly Arab Soomro and Samma chieftains; Mongols came from the east, Tartars from the north, and Turks from the west. The last to come were an unusual people called the Moghuls, who were, in fact, a Persian-speaking clan of Turkish extraction living in and around the eastern Caucasus. There was no Moghul country as such, but a number of city-states and principalities of that area were ruled or inhabited by these people. They did not call themselves "Moghuls" (it is doubtful that they had a name for themselves); the word was an Indian corruption of "Mongol," since they were believed locally to be an offshoot of the legendary hordes of Genghis Khan. They ruled kingdoms as diverse as golden Samarkand and tiny Farghana (this latter principality is located in what is now the Uzbekistan Republic of the Soviet Union).

Toward the end of the fifteenth century, the ruler of Farghana died in a fall from his polo pony. His twelve-year-old son, the prince Zahir-ud-din, succeeded him to the throne and was given the kingly name of Babar (the Lion). In Babar's own family, there was indeed Mongol blood; his father had been a lineal descendant of the great Genghis Khan himself. His mother was a great-granddaughter of Tamerlane the Mighty, and the courtiers of Farghana were astonished when their young king, with the blood of two such legendary warriors in his veins, showed a marked preference for poetry over polo or military exercises. Babar's uncle, the regent, dethroned him and expelled him from Farghana before he was eighteen. With Babar into exile went a group of loyal nobles and their men, to be hunted and hounded by the armies of the usurper. Wandering in the mountains changed Babar from poet to general. For most of his years, he was an adventurer. He and his band took and ruled various kingdoms at various times, including his native Farghana (recaptured from his treacherous uncle), before themselves being dislodged.

Near the end of his life, Babar rose from the status of military adventurer and occasional king to become an emperor and the founder of one of the most illustrious ruling dynasties in Asian history. Having consolidated a substantial kingdom for himself in most of present-day Afghanistan, Babar sought entry into the subcontinent. Two incursions were repulsed, but in 1523 he made a secret pact with the governor of Punjab. This worthy, impressed with the way the Moghuls had taken the Afghan provinces of the Delhi sultanate he served, saw an opportunity for himself in the event of Moghul success in the subcontinent. He thought that plunder was Babar's main interest and that he would withdraw once he had sacked Delhi. In the process, the power of the sultan would have been broken, and a governor might become a king in his own right. At his invitation, and forearmed with intelligence gained from him, the Moghuls came through the Khyber Pass again. They brought with them Babar's military innovations of rapid cavalry pincer movements and light field artillery. They met some resistance in the hills, but marched unmolested across most of the Punjab and on to Delhi. On the plain of Panipat, a few miles northwest of Delhi, they met the massive army of Sultan Ibrahim Lodhi, emperor of Hindustan. Ibrahim's army was at that time the largest in Asia. It was believed to be an irresistible juggernaut; Ibrahim's elephant-mounted cavalry alone outnumbered Babar's entire host twice over. But the elephant, for all its awesome strength and ponderous weight, is a slow-moving animal, and its hide is vulnerable to rockets and small cannonball. Babar's cavalry, on its fast little ponies, hemmed in Ibrahim's hordes. His artillery, musketeers, and swordsmen decimated the enemy force. Sultan Ibrahim fell in the fighting, and Babar finally entered Delhi as emperor of Hindustan.

The four years of his rule were a stormy period of military consolidation. The Moghul kingdom he established survived in various forms until 1857, except for a brief reemergence of the Afghans under Sher Shah Suri that interrupted the reign of Babar's son and heir, Humayun. It was in the latter part of the seventeenth century, during the reign of the sixth Moghul emperor Aurangzeb Alamgir, that the empire achieved its apotheosis territorially, if not intellectually. At this time it covered the entire subcontinent, the only time in history that South Asia has been governed as one country (a similar claim is sometimes made for the last days of the British Raj, but there were important exceptions then). Also included were Afghanistan and much of Burma. But the stress points were already visible: A strong personality like Aurangzeb could hold this vast, heterogeneous, and frequently rebellious entity together; his successors, effete and inept, could not. The Moghul Empire came apart, piece by piece, as ambitious governors or rebellious Hindu chieftains took advantage of the increasing weakness of the court at Delhi and set themselves up as kings.

Unused to the responsibilities of hereditary power (they had been civil servants or rebels, not feudal lords), uncomprehending of its sheer potency, these new nawabs and rajas tended to be indolent and irresponsible. They also tended to be greedy; the land was impoverished to pay for their extravagances. Their armies were undisciplined and incapable of defending the subcontinent against alien marauders like Nadir Shah and Ahmed Shah Abdali (Durrani), who came after the plunder available to anyone in the social and political anarchy that prevailed in the eighteenth century. The Moghul emperors at Delhi (incumbents changed with bewildering frequency) found themselves ruling an ever smaller kingdom. Formally, the Moghul Empire lasted until 1857, when the British discontinued their pension to Bahadur Shah Zafar, the last Moghul emperor. This hapless individual had ruled a kingdom little larger than his courtroom before the rebels of 1857 adopted him as a symbol of legitimacy during the War of Independence. Exiled to Burma afterward, he wrote some of the most excruciatingly beautiful poetry in the Urdu language.

Zafar's cousin Nawab Wajid Ali Shah of Oudh was a connoisseur of perfumes. His mission in life was the collection and enjoyment of rare and delicate fragrances. The story goes that the British discovered an unsuspected talent for potentially troublesome intrigue in this otherwise effete lord, and decided to have him assassinated. Conventional murder methods were tried, and they failed. Wajid's palace was completely protected by loyal men and no one bearing a potential weapon could enter. His food and drink were tasted by others before he would touch them. Finally, they conspired with a refuse collector in his palace and arranged to expose Wajid's delicate nostrils to the smell of human excrement. The shock was too much for this exquisitely nurtured lord; it killed him. The last well-known descendant of the Moghuls was the Nizam of Hyderabad, whose personal collection of precious stones alone qualified him for inclusion in the ranks of the world's twenty richest men in the 1950s.

PIRS, FAKIRS, AND DERVISHES

A warrior may conquer territories, administer them, and extract tributes and taxes. He cannot easily conquer the minds and hearts of men, or bring them to believe in his own religion. There is a sometimes-cited distortion of history that conversion from Hinduism and Buddhism to Islam took place at the point of a sword. The image of the "fierce, warlike Mohammedans" may have some historical justification, but whatever limited relevance it has is to the period of the Crusades rather than to the early spread of Islam. In the subcontinent, certainly, Islam was not forced on an unwilling population.

There are today some 165 million Muslims in the countries of the subcontinent. The vast majority are descendants of converts from Hinduism and Buddhism, although there are also many descendants, in varying mixtures, from the "original" Muslim nationalities (Arabs, Persians, Afghans, Turks, Moghuls). It would have required peculiarly efficient sword-wielders and remarkable means of thought control to convert nearly a third of the people of an area as vast and heterogeneous as the subcontinent by threat or legislation—and to ensure that they and their children stayed converted. Some forced conversions did occur; for example, those of certain prominent Hindu chieftains and princes humbled in battle by overzealous Muslim captains. But these converts usually reverted to their original faiths as soon as their conqueror had returned to his capital. And ambitious men may have embraced the faith of their monarch of the moment in order to advance their careers.

Such conversions are noted in history because chieftains and courtiers are the protagonists of historical narratives. But many millions of those who fought no battles, built no palaces or empires, plundered no cities—the ordinary inhabitants of town and village—became Muslims. They were neither humbled princes nor opportunistic courtiers. Their conversion to Islam was voluntary and self-sought, as are all genuine conversions to any faith. They were brought to a comprehension of this new faith by the activities and precepts of missionaries, but missionaries of a kind almost unknown to other religious groups. The Muslim saints—the *pirs, fakirs,* and *dervishes*—were unique and beautiful men.

One cannot, of course, group them together like this and discuss them as if they were a single phenomenon. They came to the subcontinent at different times over a period of some ten centuries, and many of the later saints were born there; they were different individuals, each with his own contribution to human perception of the divine. But they had many characteristics in common. They were pirs (saints), fakirs (wandering mendicants), and dervishes (a term used incorrectly in the West; it means ecstatic mystics). The early saints, some of whom preceded the arrival of the first Arab or Afghan soldiers, wandered into the subcontinent from the deserts of the Arab lands and the mountains of Persia. From the vantage point of our worldly times, they were odd, eccentric men. The vast majority were mystics. Many belonged to the Sufi sect of Islam, or were its forebears or fellow travelers; frequently they were homeless wanderers (or rather wanderers who found home anywhere they could pause for contemplation).

Seemingly aimless wanderings through towns and villages, meeting people, pausing to meditate on God and the meaning of the beauty of His creation ("If this is all mortal and transient, then why the ineffable loveliness of life and nature that hold us from Heaven?") in odd out-of-the-way places—these appear to have been common to the life styles of the different saints. Their shrines were built by disciples wherever they happened to be at the time of death. There are saints who were wild and wooly men perched on desolate mountaintops contemplating a thunderstorm and then coming down to the people in the valley to tell of their discoveries; there are saints who created music and sang divine odes. There are metaphysical philosophers who puzzled over the relationship between man and God, groping toward a moment of comprehension.

The Sufi says that soul and body will be united with God, but not in the sense of absorption into the demiurge; Muslim mystics are not pantheists and do not accept the annulment of the unique and individual psyche. This is a union of entities. The Longed-for, the Essence of all Desires, will welcome the one who has waited for the moment of ultimate communion, as the bridegroom welcomes his bride. This will happen in its own time: each mortal will stand his turn in the celestial chambers and be granted his brief glance at the Face that is the Fountain of All Light. This will happen of itself in the processes of eternity; the time will be determined by considerations incomprehensible to us. There is nothing we can do to hasten that moment or know of it in advance. Until then, we must seek to earn that moment by the practice of love for our fellow mortals, even for those whose creeds may differ from our own; for all seek the same goal by many paths. We must live our time on this earth as the One wishes of us, in order to earn His love—and He wishes lives of virtue and good works; not the mere avoidance of evil, but the positive advancement of good.

The Sufi neophyte will query his teacher: "What about the yearnings of the soul in the meantime? What of these wings trying to beat upward and out into the Light of the Universe, but constrained, imprisoned, by the surrounding flesh?" The teacher will answer: Still it by contemplation. Examine a dewdrop; look into the soul of your brother. Look deep inside your own soul. But think. Open your mind that it may reach through the universe to God. Meditate, and wait for the sudden moment of ecstatic clarity that may come to anyone—the bright strand of comprehension falling in a brilliant instant through what the human mind can observe or, observing, understand.

Different saints approached their message from different premises. Each perceived his own moment of comprehension and communicated to his disciples his own message of divine love. God-lovers and God-seekers, some among them were stern patriarchs, while others were ecstatic vagabonds. They were scholars, musicians, composers, and even dancers; they were poets. Some engaged in the more mundane occupation of politics, bringing their belief in love and tolerance to the practice of statecraft. It was not difficult for men such as these to win converts in their wanderings.

One such person was the great Amir Khusrau. This extraordinary man was an administrator, a philosopher, a linguist, a poet, a scientist, and a musician. Not considered a saint himself, he was a contemporary and a disciple of the thirteenth-century mystic known as the Pir of Herat. As a student and chronicler of the languages of the Indus Valley, Khusrau felt the need for a language that would be accessible at least to the various nationalities at the Delhi court. He patronized and contributed to the development of a kind of subcontinental Esperanto, which he called "Hindustani." In the course of history two languages have developed from Khusrau's Hindustani: Urdu, the national language of Pakistan, and Hindi, the national language of India. Yet even this is not where Khusrau's most enduring fame lies.

He loved music passionately, and was a singer of some renown himself. He was also the inventor of the well-known string instrument called the *sitar*. Khusrau became interested in the melodic structure of Hindu temple chants and the rhythms of the folk music of the Indus Valley, particularly of Sind. He secularized the Hindu hymns by the simple expedient of omitting the words, then worked the lines of the melody into the complex rhythms he developed from folk music. Over the years, he evolved a style of music that involved an exploration of the material possibilities in a single theme (or *raga*) within the confines of a subtle rhythmic structure. This is, of course, the entire concept and basis of the music of the subcontinent (what is called in the West Indian classical music). The definition of its disciplines, modes, and forms was largely the work of this one individual. In the process of his work, he also collected and composed the majority of the ragas on which this music is based.

History can produce many ironies. Muslim saints were seldom celibate, and most of them produced children and grandchildren. In the absence of a property-owning aristocracy, many *makhdooms* (descendants of saints) assumed a status not entirely dissimilar to that enjoyed by feudal lords in other societies. The tax-free land held in tithe to maintain the shrines of their great ancestors and the offerings brought there by devotees became sources of personal wealth that could be passed on to an heir, since technically it belonged to the shrine and not to the makhdoom personally. The belief of unlettered people in the powers of a saint made them loyal followers of the saint's "successor" and useful for political purposes. The inheritance of the makhdooms from their saintly ancestors was thus personal wealth and political power, with their corollary of a capacity for oppression. In the social anarchy of the Moghul decline, in the vacuum of royal decay and aristocratic ineptitude, the makhdooms gained immense influence, particularly in Sind and southern Punjab. There were instances of this power being used for benign or humanitarian purposes, but these are exceptional.

THE RAJ

Queen Elizabeth I had addressed a letter to her Moghul contemporary that annoyed the great Akbar. Through ignorance of protocol, the lengthy and sonorous list of the Emperor's titles had been written in the wrong order, thus inadvertently slighting him. In Elizabeth's letter, the Emperor's first name was misspelled to mean a word for "laxative." The first English ventures into India in search of trade and concessions met with no instant success. In 1609, an adventurer named Captain William Hawkins reached the court of Akbar's son and successor, Jahangir. Taking a liking to the plain-spoken Englishman, Jahangir invited him to one of his days-long drinking parties. Hawkins was a sturdy English sailor. He had roughed it on long voyages, and his habit of doing without a daily bath, even now that he was on land, was a standing joke at the Moghul court. He had drunk the vilest of beverages with the toughest of men; but Jahangir's exceptionally potent brew made him sneeze, then cough, and eventually pass out, while the Moghul courtiers continued their carousing for several days. Jahangir smiled. He was pleased. Having drunk Hawkins under the table at the very beginning of the party, he felt more secure in his dealings with these strange people from across the seas. James I sent an official embassy under Sir Thomas Roe a few years later, but although Roe did gain trading concessions, he did not get the commercial treaty he had been sent to obtain.

Over the years, other Europeans—the French, the Dutch, the Portuguese—also gained trade footholds. In the chaos of the eighteenth century, the subcontinent became a battleground for the various trading companies, who used individual princes to fight their trade wars for them. The most powerful such company was the British East India Company, with its principal offices at Calcutta in Bengal. In the 1750s, the company engaged in a running dispute with Siraj-ud-daulah, the nawab of Bengal, that resulted in his defeat in battle by an ambitious upstart named Robert Clive, who had obtained the assistance of Siraj's general, Mir Jafar. Then in 1765, in the Treaty of Allahabad, Clive, now the administrator of Bengal, got the Moghul emperor to give the East India Company the *diwani* (revenue control) for Bengal, Bihar, and Orissa. A new dimension was added to British activity. The foundations of the British Empire in the subcontinent had been laid, and its methods of operation established. Playing off one ruler or nobleman against the other, the East India Company gained control of most of the subcontinent in the second half of the eighteenth century. In the first half of the nineteenth century, it annexed the regions of the Indus Valley.

Punjab and the north of the Indus region had long been an area of instability and confusion. This was the pathway along which invaders from Asia traveled on their way to Delhi, and each new invader found both supporters and opponents among the Punjabi nobility, who were the administrators of the richest single province in the region. An aristocrat could easily be tempted to expand his domain by poaching on that of another; an invader found it easy to get his way by exploiting rivalries and cracking noble heads together. Believing he could serve his ambitions with the aid of a militarily powerful adventurer (a Genghis Khan or Mahmood Ghazni or Babar or Nadir Shah), a governor would assist the invader. Delhi would be sacked yet again, and the governor beheaded as a reward for his assistance. Punjab was a magnet, drawing in adventurers from the northwest and changing the history of the subcontinent. The region attained a short-lived stability in the late eighteenth century under the Sikh maharaja Ranjit Singh. He was powerful, clever, had only one eye, and was exceptionally ugly. After his death, his successors proved weak and unable to contend with the British pressure from the east.

Ranjit Singh's Sikh kingdom was one of two buffer zones between Russian-dominated Afghanistan and British-dominated India; the other was the territory of the Pathans. The latter were enemies of the British, and Ranjit was certainly no friend. He was, however, a strong monarch who cared for the Russians even less than he did for the British. He therefore could and should be tolerated. Ranjit's relations with the British were incredibly complex: It was a question of live-and-let-live, in an atmosphere of total and entirely mutual distrust.

Although the weakness of the Sikh rulers who succeeded Ranjit Singh permitted the British to pursue a more active policy in the northwest, it also worried them. The situation was too fraught with risk; weak rulers may make good puppets, but they are bad allies. So the East India Company played the same game as other invaders in the Punjab. Taking advantage of internal frictions and rivalries, they penetrated the Punjab and the settled areas of what is now the NWFP in the 1840s, though they did not formally annex the area until 1849. From here, they launched their campaigns against Sind and against the Pathan tribes on the northwest frontier. They were successful in Sind, but the Pathan mountain tribes, as always, retained their independence.

In 1843 Mir Fateh Ali Talpur, head of the federation of three chieftains who ruled Sind and most of Baluchistan, stood on the beach near Karachi and watched the beacons that told him his navy had been defeated and Manora fortress had fallen to Sir Charles Napier. The British invasion of Sind, the last successful campaign in the establishment of the British Raj in the subcontinent, was about to triumph.

Betrayed by his cousin in the north, defeated at sea, Mir Fateh Ali's time had run out. He decided to make his last stand farther inland, on the spot where his great-uncle had wrested suzerainty of Sind from the Kalhoro chieftains sixty years before. It is possible, in fact more than likely, that he stood a chance by storming the British on the beaches. But even if he could repel the beach landing, what about the troops moving toward him from the north? On the day of the battle, the mir appeared before his troops in the clothes he had worn on his wedding day, his hands and feet dyed red with henna in the manner of a bridegroom. He fell in the fighting, and Sir Charles Napier sent a one-line message to his governor: *"Peccavi"*—"I have Sind." Napier, wishing to march on Sind, had gone out of his way to provoke the mirs of that region into breaking their peace treaty with the British. Mir Fateh Ali and his cousins would not oblige, so Napier had to break the treaty himself. Napier Road in modern Karachi is named after this British adventurer. It is the street where the sailors go, the street where the city's brothels are situated.

The south of the Indus Valley had passed from the control of the Samma and Soomro chieftains to that of the Central Asian Tarkhans in the early thirteenth century. This region had been allowed to keep a quasi-independence during the days of the Afghan sultanate in Delhi; but the Moghul emperor Jalal-ud-din Akbar, known to history as Akbar the Great, had other plans. Sind came to him in the sixteenth century, with the victory of the Kalhoro chieftains over the Tarkhans. Descendants of a saintly wanderer, the Kalhoro were loyal to Akbar, and their chieftains were appointed as the Moghul governors in Sind. With the decline of Moghul power, the Kalhoro became independent rulers.

Akbar had risked nothing, sacrificed nothing, in his bid for control of Sind. Mian Mir Mohammed, the first Kalhoro prince, had taken a major gamble in enlisting the support of two Baluchi highland chieftains, Mir Aludo and Mir

Four Moghul miniatures of the seventeenth century show the blend of intricate design, sophisticated use of color, and vitality that characterizes an art form which fully reflects the divergence of cultural influences in the subcontinent.

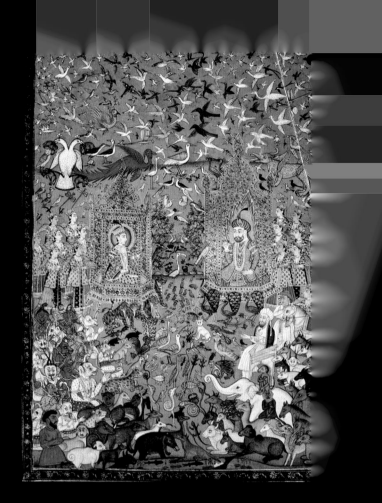

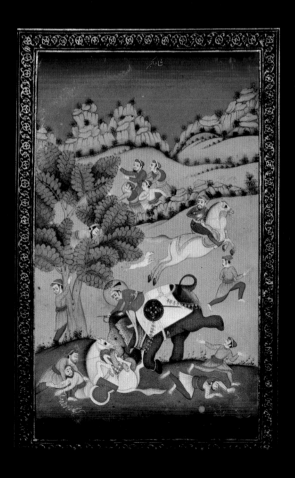

Masudo of the Talpurs. After his victory, he invited them to come and settle their people on the plains. Their arrival is described in local chronicles translated by Sir Richard Burton, the British Orientalist, who later compiled the *Arabian Nights:*

> When the Baluchis arrived within fifteen miles of Khudabad, the prince sent out several of his ministers and nobles with presents of clothes and horses with gold saddles to receive and escort his distinguished guests to the capital. As the procession advanced, it met a troop of beggarly shepherds followed by their flocks, and women mounted on asses. The ministers enquired for Mir Aludo and were much astonished when told that the ragged wayfarer with the "dheri" in his hand and the "kambo" on his shoulders was the personage whom they had been sent to conduct with such ceremony.

The ragged shepherds, with their spinning whorls and the slings in which they carried lambs across their backs, came and settled in Mian Mir Mohammed Kalhoro's plains. Two centuries later, their aristocratic descendants fought the ancestors of the prince they had aided. The Kalhoro were defeated by the Talpurs; and the Talpurs, in their turn, fell to the British on the same field.

In 1857, India reacted. Beginning with a soldiers' mutiny in Bengal, a massive series of bloody revolts broke out everywhere. The War of Independence had two main fountainheads of legitimacy. The Muslim rebels demanded restoration of the former Moghul kingdoms to the throne at Delhi, occupied for the moment by Bahadur Shah Zafar. The Hindu rebels were as much anti-Muslim as anti-British in their aims, although there were important instances of intercommunal cooperation. Using their recently created vassal-landlords, it was not difficult for the British to quell a rebellion that, though widespread and fierce, was also inchoate and disorganized. Reprisals against the rebels were exceptionally brutal and sadistic, even by subcontinental standards. The Crown took over the government of India from the East India Company; a Secretary of State for India was appointed in London, and a Viceroy in India. The Koh-i-noor diamond was added to the crown jewels. "Your Majesty," said the ever-gallant Benjamin Disraeli, bowing to his queen, "I gift you India, the brightest jewel in your crown."

THE LAND OF THE PURE

In many ways, Pakistan was an inevitable product of the advent of democracy in the subcontinent. The British had identified their own advantage in the inherent division between Hindus and Muslims. The two religions were more than creeds: They were separate ways of life, even whose secular codes were frequently opposed. Worse, Muslim kings had ruled the subcontinent for nearly a thousand years with Hindus as their subjects. "Divide and rule," decided the British; and it worked.

Nationalistic anticolonial movements broke out all over British India in the early twentieth century. Their growing popularity posed the inevitable question: "What constitutes the Indian nation? Who is an Indian?" "A believing Hindu," answered Bal Gangadhar Tilak, not stating what he intended doing with the Muslims (not to mention Christians, Sikhs, Parsees, and untouchables). Mohandas Gandhi's more mystical concept of a "Mother India" whose differing children would live as brothers was long on rhetoric and short on concrete proposals. More, his Indian National Congress party became pervaded by a distinctively Hindu consciousness and symbolism, despite its secular pretensions. Such gestures as the adoption of the xenophobic and virulently anti-Muslim anthem *Bande Matram* as the official Congress song brought little comfort to the Muslim community.

As the likelihood of British retreat from the subcontinent increased, the prospect of being a permanent minority in a dominantly Hindu India began to agitate the minds of Muslim political leaders. In the 1920s, many prominent Muslims, among them Mohammed Ali Jinnah, a Karachi lawyer, broke away from the Congress party. For Jinnah and the other Muslims who were opposed to the continuation of British rule, the dilemma was an acute one. The differences between the communities seemed irreconcilable; in a free and democratic India, the Muslims simply would not stand a chance against the simple fact of a majority of Hindus. Oppressive or discriminatory actions could be sanctified in the name of democracy by the now openly chauvinistic Congress party, notwithstanding the pronouncements of liberal socialists like Nehru.

The Muslim League had been founded in 1906 as a reformist, upper-class

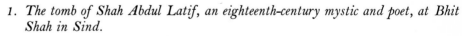

1. The tomb of Shah Abdul Latif, an eighteenth-century mystic and poet, at Bhit Shah in Sind.

2. The glazed tiles of Hala embellish mosques, shrines, and homes. The traditional patterns are handed down from father to son.

3. Wandering mendicant.

4. Village mosque, Kotha, NWFP.

5. Mosque, Chiniot.

6. Badshahi Mosque, Lahore, built by the Moghul emperor Aurangzeb in the seventeenth century.

7. Marble dome of the Pearl Mosque, Lahore Fort.

lobby for gaining concessions in British-ruled India. It had acquired a certain limited following in those provinces where Muslims did not constitute a majority because of its successful pressure for separate electorates and civil service quotas. In the Muslim-majority provinces, which are now in Pakistan, the league had made little headway, for those Muslims had no need for concession lobbies. It was not until the league was transformed into a nationalist party that it caught the popular imagination. For there was strong anticolonial sentiment among the Muslim masses as well, and it too led to the inevitable question: "After the British, what? Subjugation by Hindus?"

In the early 1930s a solution to this dilemma was posited by the poet and philosopher Mohammed Iqbal, who developed the concept of creating a separate country for the Muslims of the subcontinent. His ideas, as expressed in his verse and in his pamphlets, captured the imagination of the Muslim community, particularly in the areas which were to be the territory of the new country. Its name was to be Pakistan, the Land of the Pure. Its flag was to be a white crescent and star on a green background. The somnolent Muslim League organization was abruptly shaken awake and its machinery wrenched from the control of the vaguely constitutionalist aristocrats and "notable public figures" whose organ it had been. Now galvanized by the anticolonial Muslims, led by Jinnah and Iqbal, who poured into its ranks, the thoroughly altered league began to work for the creation of Pakistan, although this objective was not avowedly adopted until the party's convention at Lahore in 1940.

In 1947, after the Congress party had backed out of several formulas for protecting Muslim rights in the context of an undivided India (formulas the Muslim League had grudgingly accepted), Lord Mountbatten arrived from London to conclude negotiations for the transfer of power with Gandhi, Nehru, and Jinnah, the leaders of two separate mass movements. Mountbatten and the British were in a hurry to get out of India, and he had been instructed to complete the proceedings for British withdrawal by April 1948. The British left the subcontinent in August 1947, two hundred days ahead of the original schedule. Mountbatten stayed on as the first governor-general of the Dominion of India; Jinnah became governor-general of Pakistan.

Two countries came into being, and their births were accompanied by blood and violence and the most massive movement of refugees in history. The states, provinces, and regions whose populations were predominantly non-Muslim became India. Pakistan was formed from the Muslim majority areas: eastern Bengal, western Punjab, Sind, the NWFP, Baluchistan, the Baluch States Federation, Khairpur, and Bahawalpur. The fate of the people of the former princely states of Kashmir and Junagadh has remained undecided.

In the two years leading up to 1971, a fresh series of traumas shook Pakistan. There were political agitation, a military coup d'etat, civil war, and international war. In the process, the eastern province of Bengal broke away. It would be out of place to comment here on these changes; it will suffice, for the purposes of this historical introduction, to say that the land and its people are still reeling in their souls from the violence and the magnitude of these events.

2 The Land and Its People

I've wandered beggared from Tirah to Swat
Where else, my heaven, will you lead me now?
I'm like a polo ball, knocked there . . . and there . . .
And thrashed about by all the sticks of fortune.

But for one grace I thank you, heaven, still:
The flash of the Indus seen from Mir Kalan.

FROM THE PASHTO OF KHUSHAL KHAN KHATTAK

The story goes that a wandering tribe of Jews, descendants of King Saul, journeyed across the Central Asian plateaus and mountains. From the peaks of the Hindu Kush, they too saw the sudden flash of cold, clear, tumbling water.

They came down to settle along the Kabul River tributary of the Indus that flows from Central Asia through the Khyber Pass and into the subcontinent. The story is apocryphal, though it is believed by many Pathans, the people who predominate in the North West Frontier Province of Pakistan. Its supporters point to certain pseudosimilarities between Pathans and the Semitic races of the Middle East—the high, hooked noses; the prevalence of moneylending as an occupation. In fact, the Pathans (or Pashtuns, as they are also called) are derived from the ancient East Iranian population of the Sulaiman Mountains.

THE TRIBAL AREAS

These tribes—Persian-Aryan in origin—settled in the valleys on either side of the Hindu Kush and below the Sulaiman Mountains around the second century B.C. They adopted the Buddhist faith. Greek, Bactrian, and Kushan strains also passed into their ethnic makeup in the course of commerce with, and later partial integration into, the Gandhara kingdom of northwestern India.

Two distinct societal patterns developed among the ancestors of the present Pathans. In the valleys and the lower slopes of the hills, the life style was that of a semisettled pastoral people, but one organically linked to the metropolitan life styles of the Gandharan cities. The dominant ethos, like that of other early Buddhist civilizations, was quietist and contemplative. Perhaps these proto-Pathans might have continued developing, their near-idyllic existence gradually expanding to include settled farm communities and increasing integration into the mainstream of Gandharan life. This was a sheltered triangle of Asia, bounded by the Hindu Killer (Hindu Kush) range in the north, the Takht-i-Sulaiman (Throne of Solomon) mountains in the west, and the Indus River in the east. The valley in which Purushapura or Pushkalavati stood was green and pleasant and very fertile, and there were alpine slopes for grazing and temples to the Lord Buddha.

Sadly, this security was as illusory as it had proved more than once in the past. There was a gap at the head of the Peshawar valley—the gap through which the Kabul River found its way, the gap through which the early Aryans and Greeks had come: the Dara-i-Khyber. Through this gap, in the fifth and sixth centuries, poured the hordes of the White Huns. The Gandharan cities were sacked and razed to the ground. The pastoral population fled, and those who did not fly were massacred. The White Huns passed, in wave after wave, through the Peshawar valley. Crossing the Indus near Attock, they spread out onto the plains of the Punjab. The people of what is now the NWFP were driven from the valleys into the mountains, and there in the mountains were born the Pathan tribes as we know them today.

Over the course of the centuries, many came back to repopulate the valleys from which they had been driven. But they were no longer the gentle, pastoral people of before. Survival in the mountains had tempered them into a tightly knit tribal society. The new ethos was stern, austere, and patriarchal. Each tribe was a self-governing entity under an elected chieftain called the *malik*. Feuds between tribes were frequent (and occur even today), and some are known to have lasted for more than a century.

Between the ninth and twelfth centuries, the Pathan people universally shed their now-nominal Buddhism and adopted the Muslim faith. They live today principally in the North West Frontier Province of Pakistan. There are over 10 million Pathans in this province, while another 2 million live in other parts of Pakistan, principally in Baluchistan and the city of Karachi; some 3 million Pathans also live across the border in neighboring Afghanistan. Pathan culture, as it has developed to the present day, values physical strength and masculine pride. There is a strong emphasis on freedom and independence, a continuation of chivalrous traditions like the rituals of hospitality, a vocal rejection of injustice of any sort (although "justice" may be defined in ways that other societies would find hard to accept).

Younger Pathan intellectuals, growing impatient with the attitudes of their elders, sometimes argue that chivalry and pride can harden to philistinism and bigotry. They contend that emphasis on the physical has meant that Pathan artistic and intellectual institutions have remained undeveloped. It is true that there is no really substantial body of Pashto literature (Khushal Khan Khattak being an exception), but this is also true of many other folk cultures whose legends and records are handed down orally. Pathan music is melodically unremarkable, but many of the lyrics have a haunting poignancy. Their unsophisticated folk dances consist principally of wild swirlings to martial drumbeats, with the notable exception of the stately interlocking steps and movements of the dance rituals in the Kafiristan Valley.

Pathan tradition certainly includes a gun cult—a legacy of life in the mountains—and maintenance of law and order in the NWFP is uniquely difficult. Some of the greatest care and skill of Pathan craftsmen is expended on the manufacture and ornamentation of rifles. But Pathans are not lacking in other skills; leatherwork, sensuously carved furniture, pottery, fine metalwork—these are all well-established Pathan crafts. Their dominant ethos, however, remains austere and proud, their outlook on the world independent and a little narrow. And their customs reflect both this outlook and their heritage of isolation and privation.

Pathan culture and traditions are not necessarily homogeneous. Usages and customs differ among different tribes. For example, while most Pathans are rather strait-laced about sexual matters, there is the unusual method of preventing excessive inbreeding that the Kallash tribe of the Kafiristan Valley is believed to have used until quite recently. Each spring, two villages (who would have previously entered into a compact for this purpose) would hold a series of athletic competitions among their unmarried young men. The two champions, the finest examples of manhood in each village, would then be taken into the woods. Here they would be kept in complete isolation for a fortnight, and fed on honey and milk and on roots and berries believed to enhance sexual potency. They would then return from the woods, but each to the other's village. During the course of a five-day festival, each virile champion would be expected to deflower a certain number of the local virgins, and hopefully to impregnate them. The virgins thus honored would be married to youths of their village in a group ceremony on the last day of the festival, except for one, who would become the hero's bride and return with him to his village. The practice has not been followed for many years. In fact, there is little real evidence that it did exist. The Kallash are understandably wary about giving such information to "aliens," and are very jealous of their privacy.

In the "tribal areas" of the mountains (more properly termed "federally administered territories"), customary tribal law is the law of the land, whatever the legislators at Peshawar may decree. Originally, the existence of these territories was a product of the inability of the British to subdue the Pathans or merge them into British India. In order to gain military passage through the passes and defend the borders of the Raj against possible invasion from Russian-dominated Afghanistan, the British viceroys were forced to come to terms with the Pathan maliks. "Leave us alone," was the demand of the maliks. "Let us run our own lives, and you may use the passes and the roads. But if any of you sets a foot off the road onto our lands, we will shoot." So the Pathans retained their independence. The fact of exclusion from the mainstream of subcontinental economic and political life was a heavy price to pay for their independence, but most Pathans considered it worthwhile.

Pathans are known to be enterprising and earnest. They have gone out from their tribal fastnesses all over Pakistan and India in search of jobs and trade. Their sturdy physiques have won them jobs as industrial or construction laborers. Their native thrift and instinct for survival have made them fine businessmen. And, of course, Pathans recruit readily into the armed forces. In the valleys of the NWFP, where they are farmers, they have pulled yields from the relatively small area of arable land available to them that would shame farmers in more fortunately endowed parts of the country.

The majority of Pathans no longer live in the "tribal areas." In any case, even these areas are being slowly integrated into the political and social systems of the rest of the country. But the habits of mind and the social formations of tribal society continue among Pathans in the "settled" areas of the Peshawar, Mardan, Kohat, and Hazara valleys. And outside the "federally administered territories," the tribal institutions have become community institutions.

In any Pathan village or community, wherever it may be situated, however its inhabitants may earn their livelihoods, the men will gather of an evening at the *dera* (the word means simply "place"). The dera serves an essential function in Pathan community life. As a kind of men's club, it is a place where stag parties may be held. More often, it is simply a place to exchange gossip and be in the company of friends. It is a place to enjoy the ubiquitous snuff known as *niswar* and drink endless cups of heavily sugared green tea. It is a place where the bowls of hubble-bubble *hookahs* are filled and the stems passed from one man to the other. Pathan tobacco is strong and rough, but sweetened by the addition of large lumps of heavy brown sugar.

In the course of conversation, the problems faced by individual members of the community are discussed, and these discussions are "chaired" by the local malik. The community must look after its own. But the members of the community must also look to the welfare of the community as a whole. When a Pathan has committed an injustice, or even a criminal act, against another Pathan, the community will determine what constitutes a just recompense according to its own traditions and customs. A crime is not a sin, on which secular judgment may be passed and punishment visited; it is God's business to look to the punishment of sinners, in His own way and at His own time. A crime is a crime because it harms the well-being or security of the community or of a member of that community. Such harm must be redressed. If someone's wife has been seduced away, another woman must be given him from the seducer's family, or an adequate number of goats furnished to compensate him for the temporary loss of a housewife's labor and to pay for another marriage. If a man has been robbed or cheated, the felon must make up the loss by working for his victim without pay. However, a victim's right to vengeance is recognized, and is sometimes invoked. Criminal acts committed in pursuit of "justifiable" vengeance are usually condoned; it is understood that the right to extract revenge passes from father to son.

The dera is not a court, in any sense, nor does it arrogate to itself the prerogatives of a court. In the tribal areas proper, the court is the *jirga*, or "jury of elders," of each tribe; in the "settled" areas, where the great majority of Pathans now live, the normal courts of the land function. It is to these courts that a Pathan may ultimately go for justice. Most matters, however, are settled by the community itself before they get that far. The dera is a voluntary association, and it has no formal means to enforce its decisions—except by ostracism or expulsion from the community. It exists because life in the mountains was harsh and difficult. Each community had to ensure itself against potential internal friction, else the community itself might splinter and leave its members defenseless against the elements or against hostile tribes.

Though the elements are better controlled today, the dera still survives. Perhaps it constitutes an intolerable intrusion on the citizen's right to privacy; or perhaps it is a model for cooperative community living. Ask the Pathan, who is prepared to explain even the most intimate details of his private life if the members of his dera require him to and who will accept most of his colleagues' decisions, even those affecting aspects of his life with which other societies would never tamper.

The Pathan takes his dera with him wherever he goes. In the big industrial cities like Karachi, Hyderabad, and Lyallpur, where Pathans have gone seeking jobs as laborers, the dera has become a potent tool for labor organizers and trade union activists. No Pathan would dream of breaking a strike in which the members of his dera have decided to participate. In any case, if a striker's money is running low, he knows the cooperative principle of the dera will help tide him over.

WANDERING INTO SIND

Some 700,000 Pathans are believed to live in Karachi, the largest city in Pakistan. The great majority of them live a bachelor life, having left their wives and families in the NWFP—to send for, or return to, when they have made their fortunes. They now constitute the second-largest community in this "all-Pakistan" city. The largest community is that of the one and a half million Urdu-speaking immigrants from what is now Uttar Pradesh in India. There are also Gujarati-speaking refugees from Kathiawar and Bombay (though many were resident in Karachi before 1947), refugees from Bihar and Rajasthan and other parts of India, Punjabis from the north, Baluchis and Baluchi-speaking Makranis from the west, Bengalis, the "native" Sindhis, fire-worshiping Parsees, Hindus, and many other communities. Karachi, a socially and culturally complex city, is the boomtown of Pakistan. Its pre-Partition population was swelled initially by the massive influx of refugees from India. In subsequent years, people from all over Pakistan have flocked to the city, looking for jobs in the factories that mushroomed around it, or setting up trades and businesses. Today it sprawls along the Arabian Sea coast and penetrates into the lower Sind desert. It has grown out of all controllable proportions.

But although one is hard put to find people whose families lived in Karachi before 1947, there is nothing that is really young in this politically young country. In the fifteenth century, there was a prosperous little port town called Kullachi situated on what was then one of the mouths of the Indus. It was a fortified town, with two main quays, one on the river and one on the sea. There were two gates to the town. The gate by the river was called Mithadar (the "sweet" gate) and that by the sea was called Kharadar (the "bitter" or "salt" gate). The imprints of the past have a subtle permanence; even when history has been erased, the vestiges remain, the disturbed fibers of collective experience. The town of Kullachi is forgotten. Its walls have crumbled and disappeared. The boomtown of Karachi stands in its place. The Indus no longer enters the sea here, and even the sea is a little farther away. The Sweet Gate and the Salt are unknown, except to scholars. But the names of two neighborhoods in modern Karachi are Mithadar and Kharadar. They are tenement areas. Not slums; in the Orient, with its peculiar standards of human dignity and comfort, only one thing is a "slum"—a shantytown, the colonies of filthy, crowded clapboard or thatch shacks found everywhere in this city—product of the laws of economics.

Mithadar and Kharadar are not slums in that sense. The people who live in these apartments are middle-class, although the streets that wind below their balconies are fragrant with refuse and open drains. They have jobs and businesses. They are shopkeepers, produce merchants, tradesmen, jobbers—and there is even an occasional millionaire. Mohammed Ali Jinnah, the founder of Pakistan, was born in Mithadar, in a small flat in a house called Wazir Mansion. His city now sprawls across the southern tip of the Sind desert. It is an ugly sprawl of suburbs one after the other, factories, rows of workers' houses, more shantytowns, and then the farms of Malir, each with its own swimming pool and the harsh, sharp skies of the desert beyond, where broken rocks and sand dunes hide the unexpected graves and shrines of saints and chieftains whose names are now forgotten.

There is no fresh water in or near Karachi. Its citizens, the surrounding farms that feed them, and the factories in which they earn their livings, are slaked from a distance. A hundred miles to the northeast, on the Indus near the fortress city of Hyderabad, is the Ghulam Mohammed Barrage. Apart from irrigating many hundreds of thousands of acres of farmland in lower Sind, this barrage feeds a system of canals that flow south—through Kalri Lake, Haleji Lake, and Gharo pumping station—to feed the reservoirs that keep Karachi alive. Beneath Kalri Lake—a long silvery wink in the red sands of the desert—is the grave of a pair of anonymous seventeenth-century lovers. They belonged to different clans and their marriage was forbidden by their elders because of a clan feud. Their suicides ended the feud; they were buried together by the shores of the lake. The city's need for water required a larger lake, so Kalri was enlarged and the graves submerged.

There are many star-crossed lovers in the folk romances of this part of the world. Their stories are invariably tragic. The collective authors of those legends seemed to comprehend that the intensity and purity of the emotions they narrated would suffer with a happy ending; life was too real, its mundane preoccupations too urgent. Far better that the lovers should die in the prime of their youth and their beauty, before the exquisite edge of their feelings had been dulled by habit. In Sind, the best known of these love stories is the legend of Sassi and Punnu.

SASSI AND PUNNU

Sassi was the daughter of a rich Brahmin of Thatta. As a child, she was taken to the nearby city of Banbhore (whose ruins are just outside Karachi) and stood beside her father as he paid his homage to the chieftain of that city. The chieftain was entranced with the loveliness of the child and adopted her as his own daughter, a prerogative not infrequently exercised by chieftains and princes. After his death, Sassi, now a beautiful young woman, became ruler of Banbhore in her own right.

In the mountainous land of Kech, to the west of Banbhore, a serious famine occurred. Ari Jam, the Baluchi ruler of Kech, sent a deputation to Banbhore to ask for grain for his people. Sassi was sympathetic to Baluchi needs, but being a woman she prolonged the negotiations by stipulating first one condition, then another. Ari Jam's youngest son Punnu was reputed to be an exceptionally handsome young man; stories of his beauty had often reached Banbhore. The final condition Sassi laid down was that she would give them the grain only if this famed Punnu came to Banbhore. So Punnu was sent for, and his caravans eventually arrived. Sassi looked at him as he stood before her, and fell in love.

The deputation from Kech returned home with the grain. Punnu married Sassi and stayed behind in the palace at Banbhore. Ari Jam was furious when he learned that his son had married a non-Baluchi, and sent many summons to Punnu. But the young man, in the raptures of love and ministered to by his queenly young wife, ignored his father's messages. Finally, Punnu's elder brothers were sent after him. Sassi received them as guests, and lodged them in her palace. For several days, they tried unsuccessfully to persuade Punnu to return. Sassi, confident that Punnu would not leave her, did nothing to prevent his brothers from seeing him. One morning, she awoke and was told to her consternation that the camels of the Baluchis were gone. She looked in Punnu's chamber; he too was gone. For three days, she brooded on the fickleness of men, particularly Baluchi men. The attempts of her friends to console or amuse her were met only by her immense despair.

One night she decided that, faithless as Punnu seemed, she would follow him and throw herself at his mercy. Barefoot and alone, she wandered out into the desert in the track of the Baluchi caravan. But Punnu was not quite the callow and fickle young man that Sassi imagined. He had not gone willingly on the night of his disappearance. His brothers had physically overpowered him and, bound hand and foot, he had been tossed like a sack onto a camel. The Baluchi caravan, with Punnu an unwilling passenger, made its way on the long journey back to Kech. After many attempts, Punnu broke free and fled into the desert night. He headed back in the direction of Banbhore.

Sassi and Punnu wandered separately in the desert, blistered by the sun, parched by the dessicating winds. Many days later they died without ever meeting again. They could hear one another's voices calling through a howling sandstorm, but such hallucinations had not been unknown to them. They did not know that the voices they heard were real. They did not know that they were only a few yards apart, unable to see through the driven sands, when they died.

Shah Abdul Latif, an eighteenth-century mystic and the greatest of the later saints of Sind, was also a renowned poet in the Sindhi language. Most of his poems are based on the folk legends of his people, and many are sung as folk songs. In one of his songs he writes of Sassi, weeping at her trials:

Oh, grief-engendering mountain—you, my foe!
I'll speak your tale to Punnu when we meet.
The dawn brought terror, as I looked down your heights;
Your winding tracks confused me, brought deceit.
You brought no boon to help me on my way.
Your stones shrugged off the print of Baluchi feet.

Treacherous mountain, when I meet my man
I'll heap your name with all my hate and scorn.

I'll tell of how your hard rocks hurt my feet.
I'll tell of how I sat and wept forlorn
While you spared me no nightmares . . . Not a thought
Of mercy in your stony soul was born.

Oh, hateful mountain, torture me no more.
On one who suffers, let aid—not wrath—descend.
Be gracious; guide me down your fearsome slopes.
But, no . . . not you. Your jagged stones pretend
No softness to the feet of wandering girls.
You have not been, nor can you be, a friend.

Mountain, a weeping maiden sits and tells you
Her tale of absent men and love and shame.
But do you listen? Do you offer solace?
Your stones are hard; they cripple me, they maim.
Afflicted women and the mountain steep
Hide, each from each, their hearts of glowing flame.

FROM THE SINDHI OF SHAH ABDUL LATIF

SOHNI AND MAHIWAL

The southern desert, separated from the waters of the Indus by narrow strips of cultivation on either bank, and the barren mountains of Baluchistan that overtake the desert in the west are more than just the setting for the story of Sassi and Punnu. The hostile landscape, the sandstorm, the bleak distances that caravans must travel are active protagonists in the plot—as much as, if not more than, Ari Jam and Punnu's brothers. A very different setting frames the story of Sohni and Mahiwal, a legend from Punjab. In the easier climes of that region of fields and canals, the passions of the characters spin their fates; but in this tale too there is a non-human protagonist determining the shape of the plot: the river Chenab, the greatest of the five tributaries of the Indus, whose brown waters divide lovers and from whose dark clay banks potters take lumps of wet earth and mold them into sensuous forms.

Izzat Beg, son of a Moghul chieftain, rode his horse at the head of a caravan from Samarkand, traveling to Delhi with a message for the sultan and goods for trade. It was springtime, but the snows of Central Asia were unmelted. Lumps of ice still dammed the cold sprays of mountain cascades. Izzat Beg and his men made their slow way through the glacier-riven mountains and across the Afghanistan plateau. Following the Kabul River, they wound through the pass of history and into the Peshawar valley. They passed between the fruit trees laden with blossoms, the promise of what was to come. They rode over meadows of grass and poppies and wild roses. It was springtime, and this was not Central Asia.

The Moghul caravan crossed the Indus over the bridge recently built at Attock and descended stage by stage to the plains of Punjab. They came to the town of Gujrat on the banks of the Chenab. The fields of Punjab were ripening for the spring harvest; the Chenab River was full, fed by the early-melting snows of Kashmir. It flowed slowly, heavy with its fecund load of silt for the fields—so different from the foaming rills of the Moghul homeland. The journey from Samarkand had been a long and cold one, so Izzat Beg and his companions decided to rest for a few days before proceeding on their mission. The town was (and still is) famous for its pottery. Izzat Beg wandered through the marketplace to buy pots.

Unable to find what he wanted, he sneered loudly that the reputation of Gujrati wares was inflated. The merchants who heard him realized they were dealing with a connoisseur and showed him their best pieces—the ones usually hidden from tourists. This was what the Moghul was looking for, and he was satisfied. But he had begun to learn South Asian trade practices. He felt that if he held out a little longer, he would be offered even better samples of the craft of the river plains. He was still unsatisfied, he announced cannily. The merchants, puzzled by this exceptionally fussy customer, sent him directly to the most famous potter of the town. This potter's place was just outside the city, on the banks of the Chenab. He had a very beautiful seventeen-year-old daughter named Sohni, whose delicate hands were as skilled in the potter's craft as her father's. Sohni showed her father's wares to the Moghul prince. He looked at her beautiful hands; looking up, he met the glance of her dark eyes. As he took an urn from her, their hands touched.

The next day, Izzat Beg's caravan left for Delhi at his orders. Izzat Beg himself stayed on in Gujarat. Each day, he came to the potter's shop to buy, and to meet the potter's daughter. Even the wealth of a Moghul prince is finite away from his land. How many pots could Izzat Beg possibly buy? And then there were the payments for his lodgings, presents for Sohni, fodder and a stable for his horses. All these things cost money, even in those easier times, and eventually the inevitable happened: Izzat Beg was penniless. He had spent all his ready cash on Gujarat's famous pottery. But still unwilling to leave, he looked for work in the city. A pauperized prince possesses few salable skills. Izzat Beg's education had been in the crafts of a warrior, his apprenticeship had been in adjudication. What was the use of such skills to a peaceful city with no enemies and with its own elected council? In any case, the plight of this slant-eyed foreigner, who had spent all his money to meet a Punjabi girl, was a standing joke in the town. No one offered to employ Izzat Beg in any capacity.

It was the potter who eventually took pity on the prince. He hired the young man to look after the goats and buffaloes he had recently acquired. Izzat Beg changed his name to Mahiwal—the herdsman. But now the potter was confronted with a delicate situation. The prince had become a herdsman, and was no longer an eligible suitor for his daughter. And as herdsman to his own kine, Mahiwal's proximity to his daughter had increased; only the Chenab separated the pasture from the potter's shed. Sohni, the potter decided, must be married off as soon as possible. Her childhood sweetheart Dam, also a potter, had asked for her hand. Sohni's father now accepted Dam's proposal.

Sohni wept bitterly at her wedding, but brides usually weep. Dam, who loved Sohni very much, did not read in this her unwillingness to marry him. On their wedding night, while Dam slept, Sohni stole out of her new home. Taking a large baked clay urn with her, she went down to the river. She crossed the river, clinging to the floating urn and paddling with her feet, to Mahiwal on the other side. In the darkness of the river bank, she ran through the pastures to her herdsman.

These rendezvous occurred every night after that. All day, Sohni would lie in bed, disconsolate and fevered. She was obsessed; she thought only of her goatherd, came to life only at night when she ventured across the river and into his arms. Dam, who suspected but did not know what to do or say, went about tense and silent. He too was suffering, suffering the humiliation of the cuckold who does not wish confirmation. The townspeople gossiped, and their talk reached Sohni's parents. Her mother pleaded with her, but nothing could dissuade Sohni.

The gossip also reached the ears of Dam's sister, who had always disliked Sohni. She followed Sohni one night and confirmed for herself what she had heard. Triumphantly, she went to her brother and told him all she had seen: the crossing on the floating urn, the dark silhouette on the other bank, the moonlight just bright enough to identify Mahiwal. To her astonishment, the disconsolate Dam refused to do or say anything and reprimanded his sister to silence. In the meantime, Sohni's parents had given up dissuasion and resorted to subterfuge. That evening, they came quietly into Dam's house and stole the large urn she used for her river crossings, thinking she would be unable to cross without it. Dam's sister, emerging stung by her brother's reprimand, saw them take the urn. Deciding on revenge, she put an identical-looking urn in its place, identical except that the clay was still unbaked.

The potter's daughter, when she slipped out that night, should have been able to notice the switch. Moreover, she would know that unbaked clay will crumble in the water. But Sohni's thoughts were not coherent. Her mind and senses were distracted by her passion for Mahiwal. Her hands and eyes noticed nothing unusual about the urn as she placed it on the water and began to paddle out. The clay of the urn melted out into the river, swollen to a torrent by recent rains. Mahiwal heard Sohni's screams as she drowned. He plunged into the water to save her but could not find her in the blackness. He returned to the bank, stood there for a moment as he saw a shape drifting toward him in the dark current. He went out and took Sohni's water-logged body in his arms. Sohni was dead; Mahiwal's world had ended. Carrying her corpse, he waded out toward the center of the river. Only his head was above the water when the current swept his feet out from under him. Weeping and clinging to his dead mistress's body, he surrendered himself to the river.

THE LAND OF THE FIVE RIVERS

Before the advent of Islam, there were about equal numbers of Hindus and Buddhists in Punjab. There was also a significant Jain community and several obscurer faiths and sects. As in other parts of the subcontinent, the Buddhists and Jains were the readiest converts to Islam, and the Hindus followed. Large-scale conversion to Islam, particularly in the south, had begun well before the Afghan invasion.

The Sikh faith was born in the fifteenth century. It was preached by a sage named Guru Nanak (who is buried at Nankana Sahib, not far from Lahore) and made many converts from Hinduism. Sikhism is a monotheistic faith that professes to borrow from both the major religions—Islam, purged of its Middle Eastern orientations, and Hinduism without the caste system and its more "pagan" customs. In the seventeenth century, persecuted by both Muslims and Hindus, Sikhism shed the pacifist philosophy that had been part of its nascence. Sikhs, led by their militant tenth guru Gobind Singh, became an assertive, stridently nationalistic people. They grew beards and long hair to identify themselves, publicly and proudly, and adopted the generic surname Singh ("lion").

A short distance from Lahore, Guru Gobind Singh promised his followers "the whole country from Lahore to Peshawar." The Sikhs greeted this with cries of "Long live the land of five rivers." In the late eighteenth century, Punjab came under the sway of the Sikh ruler Maharaja Ranjit Singh. In the mid-nineteenth century, the British Raj extended itself over the plains and up to Peshawar. In 1947, Punjab was partitioned. The overwhelmingly Muslim western, southern, and central portions are now in Pakistan. The dominantly Sikh and Hindu eastern portions became part of India. No Sikhs live in Pakistani Punjab now. But every year, thousands of bearded, turbaned men and their families cross the border on pilgrimage to the grave of Guru Nanak. Or they come to Lahore to the white marble shrine of the Muslim saint Hazrat Data Ganj Baksh, who is equally revered by Muslims, Hindus, Sikhs, and Christians.

The ethnology of Punjab is even more complex than its religious history. These were the plains on which, since the time of the Harappan civilization, successive waves of very different peoples from Central Asia had settled and interbred with each other to produce sometimes surprising cultural fusions. The great majority of Punjabis belong to four major "native" clans (the Ja'ats, Rajputs, Gujars, and Gakhars) and a host of minor clans. A significant proportion are also of Arab, Persian, Turkish, or Moghul descent. The origin of the four main clans of Punjab is Indo-Aryan, but they include Hun and Scythian ancestries as well. These clans predominate among the country folk. Ja'ats are the largest in number; they are usually farmers, and the term "Ja'at" is often used synonymously with "farmer" and sometimes derisively to imply "country bumpkin." The Rajput tribes are the descendants of later Scythian settlers closely allied with the ancestors of the Ja'ats. Fanning out from Punjab, Rajputs have settled all over the subcontinent, particularly in now-Indian Rajasthan (originally known as Rajputana) and Uttar Pradesh.

Rajput history is an illustrious one, but frequently one of magnificent failure. Toward the closing years of the Hindu era, the Rajputs aspired to imperial control of the subcontinent. The success of the Afghan invaders, who defeated the Rajputs in battle, ended their bid for supremacy in the eleventh century. During the decline of the Afghan sultanate, the Rajputs again aspired to kingly status in India and were again thwarted, this time by the Moghul invasion. Akbar, the third Moghul, sought to salve the Rajput ego by appointing many of their chieftains to prominent positions in his government, and both he and his courtiers exchanged daughters in marriage with Hindu Rajput families. In this manner, he preempted them as a possible threat to his empire and created a privileged and loyal class of Hindu noblemen. Present-day Rajputs in India, where the majority live, are Hindu with some Sikh elements. They are heavily represented in the Indian armed forces, and a large number of Indian princes and rajas are Rajputs, a legacy of Moghul patronage in the distribution of fiefdoms. Pakistani Rajputs are those Rajput tribes who were converted to Islam between the fourteenth and seventeenth centuries. They live in southern and western Punjab and in Sind.

In the north of Punjab live the Gujar and Gakhar clans. The Potwar plateau of northern Punjab is rough country, cut into gullies and canyons by rainwater and wind. The most numerous clan living on this plateau and just below it are the Gujar, a mainly pastoral people. The "warrior" clan of the region are the Gakhar, many of whom believe themselves descended from one Kaigohar, who ruled in Isfahan in Persia and conquered Kashmir, Tibet, and part of Mongolia. They say they ruled these countries for many generations, but were driven back to Kabul by local rebels. They claim to have entered the Punjab with Mahmood of Ghazni. In fact, the story is mythical. It is not unknown for Indian peoples converted to Islam to allot themselves a Middle Eastern or Central Asian origin in their folklore.

The first subcontinental army Mahmood fought *against* before he reached the Rajput territories was a Gakhar army. The ancestors of the Gakhars were already resident in northern Punjab at the time of the Hun invasions. They were converted from Buddhism to Islam around A.D. 1200. Babar, the first Moghul emperor, fought the Gakhars before he could reach Lahore and then Delhi. In the two recorded major battles between Moghuls and Gakhars, the latter were defeated. When the Moghuls were safely in control at Delhi, the Gakhars decided to make the best of it, and their chieftain journeyed to Delhi to offer fealty to Babar.

A story has it that on this occasion, the raja of the Gakhars took an armed *lashkar* (army) with him, that being their custom. On receiving word that a Gakhar lashkar was marching toward Delhi, Babar assumed they were coming for round three of the battle. His control of India being very recent, he could not risk defeat in even a single minor skirmish. Babar pulled all his troops out of Punjab and regrouped them at Delhi to be certain of a single telling victory against the Gakhars. The raja consequently saw no Moghul troops on the way; then, to his astonishment, the Gakhars were met outside the walls of Delhi by a hail of arrows and lead. Too proud to break formation, they continued marching forward under fire. Beneath the walls of Babar's capital, with arrows, musketballs, cannon, and molten lead raining on them, they drew their swords—and held up the hilts to the men on the walls.

Babar ordered his troops to cease firing and hastily prepared a welcome ceremony with all the Moghul trimmings. The Gakhar raja entered the gates of Delhi, astounded at the fusillade followed by the sudden opening of the gates. He rode before the open-air dais where the Emperor sat. He waited, silent in his saddle, while Babar explained that, while he had naturally known all along that the Gakhars came in peace, he believed that the brave warriors who had resisted his ancestor Tamerlane would prefer to demonstrate their prowess by walking through a rain of lead rather than of roses. Now, of course, the roses would be provided. At a signal, court girls spread a carpet of petals around the hooves of the raja's horse, and court poets and musicians began the elaborate ceremonial of Moghul welcome. The raja was unconvinced by the Emperor's explanation; perhaps he was too unsophisticated. He abruptly dismounted, strode before the dais, and placed his turban at Babar's feet in the classic gesture of fealty. Peremp-

1.Tailor shop, Kotha.
2.Pathan schoolchildren, Kotha.
3.Peasant, Dir, North West Frontier Province.

torily curtailing the courtly rigamarole, he remounted and rode out of Delhi. Without having uttered a single word to the emperor, he rode back to his fortress at Pharwala (near present-day Rawalpindi), there to brood on the insult, but honor his pledge of loyalty.

The nonnative clans are descendants of Muslim settlers from the Middle East and Central Asia. Most of them trace both saints and conquerors in their lineage. There are also many people of Pathan or Afghan origin, descendants of families who came and settled in Punjab during the days of the Afghan sultanate and later. These clans, most of whom are settled in the Multan area, are thoroughly "Punjab-ized" and have long since shed Pathan customs. One exception are the Niazi, a bilingual Pathan tribe living in northwestern Punjab. In the southwest of Punjab, there also live a few small tribes of Baluchi origin. Although it is convenient to describe the Punjabi peoples in terms of clans and tribes, the social norms here are in no way those of tribal society. Clan histories are a source of myths and tales for mothers to relate to children to enthrall them with the deeds of their ancestors.

Punjab is the heartland of the Indus Basin. It stretches across the five rivers that give it its name from the foothills of the Himalayas in the north to the borders of the desert in the south.

A closed horizon—rampant blue
And blazing white—and peasant dust.
A peasant girl, escaped from heat
Bathes naked in the brown canal.

She sees our jeep. The waters close
around her dripping, sun-brown breasts.
We cross a bridge. Brown children scream
from village-safety, village-calm.

We see the fields we've come to see;
saltpeter mars a patch or two.
The tenant says the tractor has
not come to plough. We say it will.

We tell him where he should grow what.
He says he will. We start our jeep
to go on further to the next
saltpetered field by brown canal.

SALMAN TARIK KURESHI

The Punjabi landscape is varied. In the north, on the Potwar plateau, it is rocky and dry. The land is almost geometrically chessboarded by gullies and shallow ravines; the horizon is interrupted by low, brown hills and unexpected rocky outcroppings. This dry plateau, where the Gakhars and the Janjua Rajputs live, furnishes the bulk of recruits to the Pakistan army; it is the home not only of the villagers whose lives are built around their herds of sheep and their sons in the army, but of occasional bands of dacoits—bandits living the life of guerrillas in the rocky caves and gulches of the hills.

The Potwar plateau rises into the green foothills of the Himalayas in the north. The Indus runs on its west and the Jhelum River cuts across its lowest point in the southeast. Across the Jhelum, sporadic low hills decline into the Punjab plain. This region between the Jhelum and Chenab—the Chaj Doab—is the rolling pastoral country of the Gujars. Its main urban center is the town of Gujarat on the banks of the Chenab. The true Punjabi heartland begins just north of Gujarat and stretches out to the south. The plain is incredibly flat. The elevation at the highest point of each *doab* (the region between two rivers) is a mere forty feet above the level of the rivers. Here, in these brown plains, where cotton and wheat are grown, stand the principal cities of the province: Lahore, Lyallpur, Sialkot, the rapidly dwindling and dying Kasur, Gujranwala, fortress Sheikhupura famed for the flies in its marketplace, the ancient city of Multan, quaint walled Bahawalpur. In the west, the land rises briefly into the low hills beyond Sargodha and descends again into the Thal plain. The Thal was a desert until canals were dug across it some years ago. It is now sugar-cane and cotton country.

Much of Punjab was once near-desert, except for broad but nervous strips of cultivation along the rivers and around wells. The rainfall in this part of the world is not excessive, and it tends to come all at once in the five weeks of the summer monsoons. Nearly half the year is summer, and the stillness of the ele-

1

2

1. *The ritual dances of the Kafir peasants in the Kalash Valley are performed at harvest, and at weddings, births, and deaths. The movements have a peculiar swooping rhythm and the songs, an eerie, birdlike purity.*
2. *Coarse black handloom makes the loose robes of Kafir girls. Their ornaments are of old coins, hammered silver, and—strangely—also of coral and shells from the distant sea they have never seen.*
3. *Kotha landscape.*

3

ments is complete. The dust-heavy leaves of the trees do not move and people stay indoors, away from the fixed white flame of the sun in the sky. Once in a while, an incredibly fierce thunderstorm builds up. It explodes violently, lashing the trees and houses with stinging, wind-driven dust, followed by great round globes of rain. As suddenly as it arrives, the storm is gone. Brown-bodied children throw off their clothes and run outside to play briefly in the puddles and sudden rivulets. But very soon the water is gone. The land is a bone-dry ancient sponge. In the winter, the ground is white with frost and the grass breaks like glass under foot. But there are gentler interludes. Spring starts early (in mid-February) and lasts until the end of April. The rainy season in August swells the canals and rivers and brings exploring earthworms out of the ground. Early September is a balmy time, but summer returns before the month ends. November is crisp, and December and January are freezing.

To allow this thirsty land to support the 32 million people who now live on it, river-bank cultivation and irrigation from wells were insufficient. So Punjab is now criss-crossed by the most extensive canal system in the world. The first canals were dug before the Afghan sultanate, and the system reached an approximation of its present magnitude during Moghul times. The British, while dividing Punjab into provinces and states, completed the canal system. Since 1947, because of the division of river waters between Pakistan and India (the bigger neighbor extracts almost all the water from the three southern rivers—the Ravi, Beas, and Sutlej—before they reach Pakistan), many more canals had to be dug to transfer water from the northern rivers into the canal systems fed by the southern rivers. The rivers of Punjab flow approximately southwestward. The major canals run transverse to this flow. This transverse direction cuts across the Indus plain's normal direction of drainage and introduces its own problems. Water follows its normal flow and seeps through the western banks of the canals. Over the centuries, it has built up against underground rocks. In many places, it rises to just below the surface and rots the roots of standing plants. Deep lodes of underground salts are tapped by the water and rise to the surface. The water evaporates, leaving a fine layer of saltpeter in which nothing can grow. As a consequence, many Punjabi farmers are returning to well water for their lands—to diesel-driven tube wells, used as much to lower the level of subsoil water by pumping it back into the nearest canal as to irrigate the land.

In southern Punjab, occasional sand dunes and unexpected patches of thorn-clad barren soil obtrude into the canal-fed fields, reminders of what the land was and could become again. Such dusty omens occur all over Punjab, but in the south they multiply, increasing in number as one travels, until the sand stretches from horizon to horizon. This is the Cholistan desert that broods along the southeast of the Punjab and into Indian Rajasthan. It is a bleak place, where even the scrubs are few. The people in the small towns that dot the Cholistan perimeter are terse and unfriendly. In the desert, occasional bands of nomads, lonely in the vast bleakness, wander from one oasis to the next.

The medieval Jain sage Dakshiniyachina wrote of the people of Punjab and described their principal qualities as "courtesy, fortitude, erudition, and mercy." Their more urbane neighbors from what is now Uttar Pradesh in India, on the other hand, have been known to characterize Punjabis as swaggering louts, and there are those among them who have contended that "the only culture Punjab has ever had is agriculture." As the most obviously prosperous inhabitants of the country they live in, Punjabis are bound to draw a great deal of comment from people of other areas. If there is such a thing as a Punjabi personality, it is found in the traditional vigor of a people whose ancestors impregnated a near-desert with water and sweat to create the breadbasket of a subcontinent. In this region, the values that are stressed are frequently energetic rather than contemplative. But the charge of anti-intellectualism can scarcely be laid against cities like Lahore and Multan (and even fabled Delhi was once a part of Punjab), which have been centers of science, scholarship, literature, and music for centuries.

The most noticeable Punjabi characteristic is the immense importance of interpersonal frankness and honesty, which is elevated almost to the level of ritual—and sometimes a ritual of rudeness, the language being earthy and replete with fragrant obscenities. Punjabi is based on various ancient Prakrits of the region, strongly influenced by Persian and various Central Asian tongues. Exceptionally rich in dialect variations, it is said that "Punjabi is a different language after every thirty miles."

Multan, the cultural center of south Punjab, was an old city at the time of Alexander's invasion. Outside the then city, Alexander fought the Malli tribe (the Muslims, in later centuries, called the region "Malli-astan"), and was seriously wounded in battle. During the Hindu era the city enjoyed little importance and fell into decline; but it became a center of commerce and culture after the early Arab conquests. It flourished during the time of the Afghan and Moghul empires. Unlike most other subcontinental cities, it did not decline during the anarchy of the eighteenth century, for Multan had been, by chance, the birthplace of the invader Ahmed Shah Abdali (the founder of the state of Afghanistan) and enjoyed his potent military protection and economic patronage. But it did decline in the time of the Sikh kingdoms and the British Raj. The British campaign for neighboring Sind was launched from Rajputana and Bombay; in Punjab itself, their attentions were concentrated on the road that ran from Lahore to the Khyber. With little to offer the Raj, Multan and its prickly, proud inhabitants were left alone. The city stagnated, brooding on its old-time splendor, until the creation of Pakistan.

Multan today is a major industrial town—but, more important to many, it is a center for music. The old noble families of the city, descendants of ancient saints, are neither as wealthy nor as politically dominant as they once were; but the tradition of supporting and patronizing musicians survives here, to the enrichment of Pakistani classical music. The musicians live in the narrow, winding lanes inside the walled city's Harem Gate. The houses of renowned artists are interspersed with the apartments of dancing girls and pop musicians. And all around are the balconies from which, since ancient times, practitioners of the world's oldest profession have beckoned to their patrons.

The city is dominated by the blue-tiled dome of the shrine of Shah Rukne Alam, the eleventh-century patron saint of Multan. Just below it is the tomb of his father, the saint Ghaus Bahaw-al-Haq. The tombs are at the highest point in the city, on a hill inside the fort that was later built around them. The electric blue of their tilework, visible for many miles, is also a symbol of the best-known craft of Multan. The blue and white tiles that decorate houses, mosques, and monuments are a hallmark of the city. Moghul nobles became fascinated with another traditional Multani craft, that of *shishagiri* (designs made from mirror fragments), and the domed interiors they had built in their pleasure houses are covered with tiny mirrors in intricate designs. A single lamp would light up the entire dome, or a torch, swung around once, would create light-echoing fantasies of reflection.

CITY OF A HUNDRED GARDENS

The favorite Moghul city was Lahore, queen of the cities of the subcontinent. Lahore has known many dynasties and many cultures. It has been the capital of all the Punjabi kingdoms there have been, and the provincial capital of whichever empire Punjab was part of at any time. It was the capital of the first Afghan sultanate of northern India before the Afghans moved to Delhi. In the time of the Moghuls (whose first capital was Delhi, then usually Agra, and finally Delhi again), Lahore enjoyed the special status of second city. In the seventeenth century the fourth Moghul emperor, Jahangir, brought his court here for a time. Whatever the benefits of Moghul imperial residence may have been, Lahore attained its cultural apex during the time Jahangir and his equally famous second wife Noor Jahan (Light of the World) ruled India. It was an apex of cultural and intellectual activity from which Lahore has never declined, although there were frequent lootings and sackings in the eighteenth century. Even today, it is the center of university life and artistic and intellectual activity in Pakistan.

Jahangir had a deep emotional attachment to Lahore. As a youth, when he was merely Prince Salim and had not yet assumed the awesome title of Jahangir (World-shaker), he visited the Mela Chiraghan (Festival of Lamps) held every spring in Lahore. He noticed a very beautiful girl standing by a tree. As an excuse for speaking to her (even a Moghul prince must find a plausible pretext), he asked if she would hold the two prize pigeons he had brought with him. He left her for a few minutes, to watch a wrestling match; when he returned, he was surprised to see that the girl held only one pigeon. "What happened to the other one?" demanded the angry prince. "It flew away," said the girl. "How did it fly away?" questioned the prince. "Like this," said the girl and released the second pigeon. The prince was amazed that someone could be so impertinent to royalty, and so careless with royally bred birds. But he did not know whether to be annoyed or impressed.

Much later, on another visit to Lahore, he was being entertained by a troupe of dancing girls. Among them, he recognized his girl of the pigeons. In the days that passed the prince spent all his time with the beautiful dancer, whose name was Anarkali (Pomegranate Blossom). One night, in the myrtle-scented pavilion of his apartments in Lahore Fort, he declared his love to Anarkali and asked her to marry him. The declaration and proposal were overheard by Jodhabai, Salim's stepmother. She wrote about the affair to Salim's father Akbar, who ruled India at the time. The great Moghul's rage shook the empire. His son marry a dancing girl? Never. Salim was bewildered. He did not wish to be a bad son to his father, but he loved Anarkali. Simultaneously defiant and confused, he held to his resolve. Dissident chieftains and nobles, learning of the quarrel in the royal family, encouraged Salim to revolt against his father and cut Punjab away from the empire.

Akbar journeyed to Lahore, ostensibly to try and resolve matters. In reality, he had conspired with Jodhabai. That evening, the Great Moghul asked for Anarkali to entertain him. Salim, thinking this the first sign of paternal unbending, readily agreed. As planned, Jodhabai had filled Anarkali's cup with pure alchohol a little prior to the scheduled performance. The girl was drunk and oblivious of her surroundings; only her training permitted her to perform her dance without reeling and stumbling. But in her drunken state, the only man of whose presence she was conscious was the man who filled her thoughts—her lover Salim. At the end of the dance, at the customary bow of allegiance, she fell to her knees at Salim's feet. To declare allegiance to anyone else, even the emperor's son, in the presence of the emperor constituted a conscious demonstration of disloyalty, an insult to rank which could only be construed to mean that the rank was not acknowledged by the declarer.

"Treason," thundered Akbar. Anarkali was arrested on the spot and summarily sentenced to death. "But I am a loyal subject of the emperor," she protested. "Then prove your loyalty by doing what the emperor commands," she was told; "renounce your feelings for the prince Salim." This she was not prepared to do. She was bricked into a wall, there to suffocate to death. Even as the last bricks were being laid, the story goes, she was offered her life if she recanted. She refused. The executioners could hear her singing as they slid the last brick into place. Eventually, the singing ceased. Salim was grief-stricken, and went into a decline from which it seemed he would never recover. But recover he did, since that is the way of Moghul princes; he went on to become the emperor Jahangir. He married the shrewd and beautiful Noor Jahan, among many other wives, and had many children.

Anarkali is now the name of a bazaar in Lahore, very near the place called Anarkali's Tomb. The bazaar divides the two Lahores, the old city and the new.

Inside the walls is the incredible complex of twisting lanes and alleys that is the Old City, and the elaborately carved balconies of houses whose age is counted in generations. The new city starts outside the walls on the south and the east—although "new" in the context of Lahore is a euphemism for that part of the old town outside the walls and those portions built during the Raj. There is still another "new" Lahore: the uninspired upper-class suburb called Gulberg, the factory workers' estates at Moghulpura and Kot Lakhpat, the taut ugliness of middle-class Samanabad. These byproducts of progress are unfortunate excrescences on the face of one of South Asia's loveliest cities.

Lahore is a green and white city—green with gardens and boulevards and high, old trees arched over its roads; white with Moghul marble, myrtle and *chambeli* (jasmine) flowers, and the silver eucalyptus trees that line the canal. Here and there there is the red of the small, intensely fragrant Lahore roses and of old brick houses with rosewater-sprinkled courtyards. In every way, the city ostentatiously flaunts water. Gardens, flowers, trees, boulevards, grass, fountains: all these things seem to say, "Look. We can afford this extravagance, this prodigality. We have water; we can afford beauty and grace."

URDU

In the early years of the present century, the educated among the Muslims of Punjab decided to do something to encourage the development of a coherent Muslim consciousness in the subcontinent. Many of them believed that at least the educated should try to speak a common language, regardless of their region, and let it slowly trickle down to the uneducated. The University of Aligarh (in Indian Uttar Pradesh) had led the way in advancing Muslim education; founded in 1875, it had become the principal intellectual center of Muslim India and the nucleus for the formation of a Muslim consciousness. The Punjabi Muslim intelligentsia, many of whom were Aligarh-educated, opted for Urdu (the language taught at Aligarh) as "their" language.

An entire generation of literate Punjabis (and many Sindhis, Pathans, and Baluchis) sat down to learn this language or to ensure that their children spoke it. The college of the city of Lahore and the Punjab University became centers for the development and propagation of Urdu second only to Aligarh. The process struck deep wellsprings of identification and consciousness: In the present century, a disproportionate number of the leading Urdu authors and poets are Punjabis, for whom this is a second language. All Punjabis speak or easily understand Urdu as well as their native Punjabi, particularly in the towns. All educated people read and write in Urdu. The same is true in varying degrees of all the linguistic groups of Pakistan, and Urdu is the national language and the language of government at the federal capital of Islamabad. The people to whom Urdu is a first language are the community known as the Muhajirs (refugees). These are the people who left Uttar Pradesh in India after Partition.

Amir Khusrau's Hindustani "Esperanto" was a synthesis of various native Prakrits (vernaculars—spoken languages as opposed to Sanskrit or written language) mixed with Persian, Arabic, and some Turkish words. Over the years it evolved, in the then provinces of Delhi, Oudh, Agra, and Banares (later combined by the British into the United Provinces, and now called Uttar Pradesh), into present-day Urdu and Hindi. Urdu was spoken by the Muslim inhabitants of that region and by upper-class Hindus. Hindi was spoken by middle-class Hindus and others. Although the two languages appear to have many superficial similarities in their everyday conversational usage, they are really very different, and the difference is most marked at their literary or "educated" levels. They also use entirely different scripts: Urdu is written in a modified Persian form; Hindi, in the Sanskrit Devanagari script.

The Uttar Pradesh region was long the location of the courts that ruled the northern subcontinent, whether from Delhi or Agra or whether the empire of the day was Afghan, Moghul, or British. It was here that aristocratic patronage of scholarship, literature, and the arts was greatest, and it was these cities that were the arbiters of the old Indian metropolitan life style and values. The Muslims lived mainly in the cities and towns. This region had been the center of the old Aryan concept of Hindu India, so there had been no widespread conversion of the rural population to Islam. The Muslim-oriented urban culture that developed had obvious correspondences but few organic links with the Hindu-oriented folk cultures of the countryside.

If the towns of the UP constituted the metropolis of the old Muslim Indian cultural entity, its "suburbs" covered a vast area. In the east, they included Bihar and much of Bengal. In the south and west, there were outposts in Bombay, in many of the princely states of Rajputana, and in the distant South Indian state of Hyderabad. In the west, the principal cultural "suburb" was Punjab and its capital of Lahore. Punjab was the commercial and military corridor between the UP and the rest of Asia; it identified more strongly with the metropolis than most other regions. Although Punjabi was a vigorous and living language, the cultural emphases and formations there were very like those of the UP, but greatly enriched by synthesis with Punjabi folk cultures. Beyond the "suburbs," an important Muslim cultural province developed in Sind. This was a relatively distant part of the empire, with important historical and social patterns of its own. An indigenous courtly culture based on a refinement of folk themes developed here independently of that of the UP. Among the nonurban Pathans and Baluchis, the native folk cultures owed nothing to city tastes and preferences.

After 1947, with the partition of the subcontinent, many of the Muslims of the UP migrated to newly formed Pakistan. All the refugees did not come from the UP; in fact, the largest number were those from East Punjab. Most of the East Punjabi Muslims crossed the border to haven in Pakistani Punjab. The physical hazards and material privations they endured on their treks were nightmarish, but their sense of ethnic dislocation and cultural shock was small. The vast majority of non-Punjabi refugees (principally from the UP) settled in the province of Sind, particularly the Karachi area. The three largest cities of this province (Karachi, Hyderabad, and Sukkur) are overwhelmingly Muhajir in their ethnic makeup.

Traditional Sindhi society was the product of a stable, culturally provincial, semifeudal life style. The arrival of the Muhajirs in this region affected the ethnic balance and brought with it a socially mobile, articulately middle-class, metropolitan social ethos. For both the "new" and "old" Sindhis (the terms are a recent vogue), the cultural shock was intense. Both communities experienced a hardening of attitudes, a protective stiffening of sociocultural institutions, a strident assertion of identity. In their opposed postures of "protecting the heritage," both the Sindhi-speaking and Urdu-speaking intellectuals were unwittingly doing more harm than good to their respective languages, for assertions of traditionalism and linguistic "purity" inevitably stifle the natural living quality of any language. It was fortunate for Urdu, both as a popular spoken language (most Sindhis also speak or understand Urdu) and as a form of literary and cultural expression, that Lahore and the Punjab University existed eight hundred miles to the north of Karachi. The language survived the ravages visited on it and has remained vital and current—a viable national language for a multilingual country.

SINDHI

The Sindhi language has since come to be accepted as a language of provincial government and has won back the respectability it had begun to lose. This is a happy circumstance, since Sindhi is a rich and ancient language; to have made of it a romantic anachronism served by scholars and occasional political chauvinists would have been a major cultural loss. The Sindhi language has five main dialect variations: Lari in lower Sind, which is the basis of literary Sindhi; Tharavi in the Thar desert regions; Kutchi in the Kutch peninsula; Lassi in the coastal areas; and Siraiki in upper Sind. Sindhi derives from a late group of Prakrits called Virachada spoken by the Aryan tribes of this region in the first few centuries A.D. In its medieval and modern forms, it is heavily influenced by Arabic and some Persian. Sindhis, like Punjabis, are a dominantly Ja'at or Rajput people. But this was an area of major Arab settlements, and pronounced Semitic physical characteristics are more marked here than elsewhere.

In medieval times, Sindhi did not develop as a written language. The upper strata of society used Persian as the language of government and literature. The languages of cult were Arabic among Muslims and Sanskrit among Hindus. These were contrasted with the Sindhi dialects spoken by the bulk of the population ("the rough and low speech of the common folk") to emphasize the privileged status of the upper classes. Medieval Sindhi therefore received little of the scholarly patronage essential to its development as a language. But because the uniquely rich music of Sind was solidly based on folk themes, the language remained alive and current in the courts of merchants and nobility, and a sophisticated tradition of ballad poetry developed. The language, with indirect patronage, thus did not degenerate into a group of rough country dialects. By the seventeenth century, when Persian in Sind had begun to disappear with the decline of the urban commercial economy, Sindhi was more than able to fill the literary gap.

For three centuries prior to the refugee influx, Sindhi society had been stable and rather static. Its cultural formations (which borrowed but were quite distinct from the mainstream of metropolitan Indian life) had a uniquely rich flavor of their own. They were provincial and a little insular, although the more distinctively hued for this. In medieval times, Sindhi society had developed with an urban emphasis. The source of the region's wealth was commerce and trade, and its centers were river ports like Thatta and Sukkur (which gave access down the Indus to the Arabian Sea) and hinterland market towns like Shikarpur in upper Sind. Goods from Samarkand and the golden cities of Central Asia traveled through the northern mountain passes and down the Indus, to be sold eventually in Africa, Persia, and Southeast Asia. The silks, spices, and crafts of the subcontinent came this way (and through the port of Surat near Bombay), as did the native Sindhi manufactures of indigo and saltpeter.

The sea routes to Africa and Southeast Asia were controlled by Arab merchant fleets, who did not object to sailing up the Indus to the river ports of their Sindhi "relatives." But the times changed. Arab mercantile ascendancy became a victim of history with the rise of the Persian and then the European navies. The swordmakers of Samarkand found better markets in Turkey and Europe, as wars of various sorts became endemic in that part of the world. The carpetmakers of Bokhara became interested in the new wealth of burgeoning Europe, and samples of their craft began appearing in the homes of Italian merchant princes and Turkish potentates. Other Central Asian goods also began to find readier and more accessible markets, for the journey through the mountains and down the Indus was long and hazardous. The goods of the subcontinent moved increasingly through Surat and Bombay and the South Indian seaports, and less and less through the Sindhi river ports. The Sindhi coast offered few natural harbors, and European and Persian captains were less disposed to sail up the Indus than Arab traders had been.

World demand for goods like indigo and saltpeter, which was used for gunpowder, propped up the Sindhi commercial economy for a time, but cheaper and more convenient sources were being developed by the new arbiters of the world's destiny. History eventually caught up with Sind. The region fell into a sharp decline, victim of shifting trade routes and the changing fortunes of empires. The merchants of Sind rapidly became impoverished; and with their impoverishment, their mansions, their cities, and their culture crumbled. The Sindhi economy retreated into the countryside; in its now-shrunken form, the only producers of the small wealth of the region were the farmers. The political dominance of the cities disappeared; the new masters of Sindhi destiny were the *waderos*—the country barons of Sind.

The decline of the cities was dramatic. In the fifteenth century, Thatta was, by the standards of the times, an urban giant that housed over half a million people. In the seventeenth century, the population of the Sindhi capital was recorded at 300,000. It had shrunk to 100,0000 in the 1750s; to 20,000 in 1810; and to 7,000 in 1851. Sukkur became a ghost town that was virtually rebuilt in the nineteenth and twentieth centuries. Hyderabad, a relatively new and small town, barely survived the crash. Shikarpur became a center for money-lending and usury to finance the crops of farmers and the pleasures of their lords.

The waderos now dominated Sind's culture as well as its politics and wealth. They were the new patrons of art and music, and their tastes determined the conceptual emphases of artists and craftsmen. A pronounced bias toward and major borrowings from folk themes had characterized Sindhi artistic activity even in the days of urban patronage. This trend intensified as rural themes were refined to suit the inclinations of individual barons. Persian was now spoken only in the governmental centers (and in the homes of the Talpur mirs). The country nobles, and the poets and scholars they promoted, spoke Sindhi. The language had begun to come into its own, a trend heralded by the popularity of the *Risalo* (anthology) of Shah Abdul Latif, the great Sindhi poet of the eighteenth century.

Under the British Raj, there was a resurgence of commerce and some industry in the region. Karachi began to grow, as did the river ports of Hyderabad and Sukkur. The arrival of the Muhajirs after 1947 swelled these cities incredibly, and economic integration with the rest of Pakistan generated a new economic boom in Sind. But the semifeudal culture that had been dominant for more than three centuries had bred its own attitudes and habits of mind. Where population pressures on the land are not extreme or where the ready proximity of saintly shrines acts to reduce personal anxieties and tensions, an agrarian society is stable. To the twentieth-century mind, the obvious inequalities of a feudal order frequently constitute a negation of humane principles; but, whatever its demerits, such an order does make for a stable and secure, and therefore contented, society. The individual knows his place in the scheme of things, however unelevated that place may be; the lack of social mobility means an absence of the personal tensions and drives implicit in social ambition. Deeply felt clan ties and strong links to the land mean an absence of the insecurities generated by the migration of people in search of work and the breakup of family units.

Traditional Sindhi society, for all its obvious faults, was secure and easygoing. Today, when the last generations of the twentieth century are being conceived, the Sindhi personality continues to be characterized by an easygoing charm. There is a certain optimism that, in spite of the inconvenience of daily reality, somehow all will be well. There is an extravagance of spirit, and of money. There is a love of color and song and dance. There is a delight in sensuous enjoyment, an exasperating lack of practicality and thrift. Such attitudes contrast sharply with the cautious, work-ethic-oriented, immigrant life style of the Muhajir and settler communities in the province. The charge of being lazy and irresponsible is sometimes leveled at the Sindhi by the more competitive members of his own community.

Sindhi society is no longer stable, and has not been so for a long time. There are important population pressures on the land and on available water; feudal ties have broken down, and both the economic benefits and the psychological and social tensions of the twentieth century have come to the Sindhi inhabitants of Pakistan. Fortunately, their lightheartedness and their optimistic grace have not yet been the victims of social change. These qualities are too deeply rooted in the Sindhi psyche, as is their music, their love of saints and devotional ritual, the poetry of Shah Abdul Latif, and the *jhoomar* they dance in their villages.

BALUCHISTAN

Along the coast to the west of Karachi, the brown desert sweeps down to pale yellow beaches. Like most Pakistani landscapes, it is sere and hard. A Pakistani poet, writing in English, describes Baleji, a cliff-sheltered bay on the Baluchistan coast.

Picture such a sky,
not closed and low, like some,
                    but high
and sapphire hard.
Whole cosmic systems of forces
refined and focused down
to the single white star
of the sun.

And the sea,
beaten flat
as a brass plate.

Away from the grease-streaked air of Karachi, the sky suddenly shows itself a hard, crystal blue as one nears the border of the province of Baluchistan at the Hab River beyond Baleji. Along the coast of Baluchistan are the small, brightly colored villages of the Makranis, who give their name to this, the Makran coast.

Makranis are fishermen and small traders. At some point in time, a group of fishermen from Nubia in present-day Ethiopia sailed a little too far from shore. Their cockleshell boat, driven by the monsoon winds of the Indian Ocean, carried them beyond their horizons and eventually onto the coast of Baluchistan. That, at least, is one story; but it is a doubtful one. Another story has the ancestors of the Makranis being brought over as slaves by Arab traders. Another suggests they were a group of African traders who took advantage of the short-lived Pax Arabicus and came to India. Yet another theory-legend suggests an East African colonial expedition in pre-Arab times; still another makes the settlements a byproduct of the commerce between the Harappan cities and ancient Egypt.

All these theories and tales are meant to explain the startling racial difference between the Makranis and all other peoples of the subcontinent. The populations of the subcontinent are predominantly Caucasian with, in various parts, Semitic or Asian racial mixes; or they are Dravidian. The Makranis are neither Caucasian, nor Dravidian, nor mongoloid. They are markedly a Negroid people, with complexions, hair, and features similar to those of the peoples of northeast Africa. Although the various theories seek to explain this racial phenomenon by ascribing the Makranis an African, not an Asian, origin, there have recently been some archeological and anthropological signs that a race of Hamitic or Negroid people may once have been native to this part of the continent. This was before the epoch when the populations of the world began their vast movements, and would have been even prior to the advent of the Dravidians in the northern subcontinent. It is possible that the Harappan cities maintained links with these people and that they themselves attained a substantial level of advancement. If their present-day remnants are the Makrani people, they are the oldest race on the subcontinent of South Asia, and one of the oldest settled communities in the world. They live mainly along the arid Makran coast of Baluchistan. There is also a sizable Makrani community in Karachi and occasional Makrani villages on the Sind coast.

To the north of the Makran coast, the land becomes rocky and rises into the dry hills and mountains of the region of Baluchistan known as Kalat. In these hills live the Brahui (gypsies), the people whose language is the only remnant of Dravidian in the northern subcontinent. Arid, mountainous Baluchistan is in area the largest province of Pakistan (nearly half the land area of the Indus Basin region) and by far the smallest in population. Fewer people live in this immense territory than in the city of Lahore. Moreover, they consist of five sharply distinct ethnic communities: the Negroid Makranis, the Dravidian Brahuis, the Caucasian Baluchi (the largest single community, who give the region its name), the little-known clan called the Hazaras, and the large Pathan community.

The Baluchi language, which is spoken by Baluchis and Makranis, has Persian roots. Its dialects are also spoken across the border in Iran, where there is a large Baluchi community. The Baluchi dialects are most Persianized in the far west, on the borders of the Iranian province also called Baluchistan. In central Baluchistan, Brahui words and phrases are freely incorporated; in the east, Baluchi blends with Sindhi, with Pashto in the north, and with Jatki Punjabi in the northeast. The Brahuis speak their own distinctive language, although most of them also speak Baluchi. The clan of the Hazaras, who may be a remnant of the hordes of Genghis Khan, are a Mongol people living in the far northwest corner of Pakistan. They speak a variant of Turkish, and often Farsi (Persian). The Pathan inhabitants of Baluchistan are native to the mountains that separate this region from Afghanistan, and speak Pashto.

In the first half of the first millennium A.D., the ancestors of the Baluchi were a group of Indo-Aryan tribes living in these hills. To the west lived various Tajik-Iranian tribes, separated from the Aryans by the Brahui settlements. In the sixth and seventh centuries, an eastward migration of the Iranian tribes, which skirted the Brahui territories, took place; they settled alongside the Indo-Aryan tribes and intermarried with them. This particular fusion gave birth to the Baluchi ethnolinguistic community. Their province is the most backward part of Pakistan, both socially and economically. In these arid mountains, settled cultivation has not been possible until recently. The dynamics of society as we know it appear to depend on the development of Neolithic farming settlements at some point in a people's history, or the emulation of the ways of a settled civic order. Such developments did not occur among the Baluchi. Their life pattern (and that of the Brahuis and Hazaras) still revolves around their herds of sheep and goats, whose flesh they eat and whose hides they sell or exchange. With their flocks they wander from one thorny pasture to the next. Their life style is that of near-nomads, and their social organization is rigidly tribal.

Each tribe has its own *tumman*, or living area, an expanse of land within which the members of the tribe roam in search of pastures, and woe betide the man whose flocks stray into the tumman of another tribe. The tribe is headed by a hereditary chieftain called the *sardar*. Tribal jirgas here—far from being democratic juries of elders, as in the Pathan regions—tend to be councils of the sardars. Such a rigid system makes for a highly dispersed society. Tribal exclusivism results in ethnic exclusivism, and the sharp definition of the five ethnic groups of Baluchistan. The fusions of races and cultures that have characterized other regions of the Indus Valley were not a feature of Baluchistan. Most Baluchis seldom marry outside their tribes and never outside their own ethnic communities; the only exceptions are the occasional intermarriages between certain Brahui and Baluchi tribes. Tribal Baluchistan has its own unusual folk flavor. Its syncopated, strangely intense folk music is very different from the lyrical lightness and effortless melodic complexity of Sind to the west, and totally other to the rhythmic exuberance of Punjab.

Baluchi history has usually been a subtheme in the history of Sind, and to some extent that of Iran. But in recent years, Baluchis have begun to come into their own. The stern rigidity of tribal practices, engendered by the very act of survival in a rocky land, is a dying phenomenon. Mining entrepreneurs have begun to pull open the Baluchistan hills. Major deposits of natural gas are being exploited, and it is believed there is oil somewhere. Some canals have been dug, and there is a limited amount of cultivation. Baluchi tribal society has outlived its utility.

THE MOUNTAINS OF THE NORTH

The Baluchistan plateau is not completely dry. There are many smaller and greater rivers: strange streams that start proudly from the sides of mountains, only to peter out in great mud valleys two hundred miles from the sea; rivers whose gurglings can be heard deep underground somewhere and that appear from caves for a bright mile or two before disappearing underground again; rivers whose course is unpredictable, one season through one valley, the next through another. It seldom rains in Baluchistan. When it does, up in the mountain catchment areas, sudden flash floods race briefly across valleys and flats over a hundred miles away. The wind-eroded mountains flash every conceivable color—the blue of copper, the red of iron, the yellow of sulphur, the orange of chrome. The bright metallic core of each mountain has been stripped of its covering of earth and boulders, and stands exposed to the gaze of prospectors.

In the north, the valleys of Quetta and Ziarat are clothed with fruit trees—gift of a stray gust from the monsoon that periodically comes this way and rains itself out in these mountains. The range bends northeastward from Baluchistan and rises through the NWFP. At the end, in the far north of the Pathan lands, it joins the Pamir knot. This is the fabled Roof of the World. From the Pamirs, the great mountain systems of Asia radiate in four directions: The Himalayas to the east and the Hindu Kush to the south (sheltering the South Asian subcontinent between them); the Sulaiman to the west and southwest and the jagged Karakoram and Caucasus to the north and west. The Pamir knot separates Pakistan from Afghanistan, China, and Soviet Central Asia; its peaks include eight of the world's ten highest mountains.

The far north of Pakistan is a land of five-mile-high mountains and almost inaccessible valleys. The people of these northern valleys speak variants of the Kohistani group of Pashto dialects. They are ethnically Pathans, but the isolation and inaccessibility of each valley has, over the centuries, resulted in uniquely inbred histories and the development and survival of odd customs and social forms. Kafiristan—the land of the *kafirs*, or infidels—for example, is one such valley, where strangely altered remnants of pagan Greek rites survive among the religious rituals of these nominally Muslim people. In the valley of Hunza, which tourist pamphlets call Shangri-La, the institution of private property is still unknown, and a primitive cooperative community exists. In Gilgit, the inhabitants invented polo, which they play on fast little ponies that arrived here no one knows when or from where. The largest and best known of the valleys below the Himalayas is Kashmir. But that, of course, is an entirely different story.

In the house where the old man lived
the walls were red sun-baked bricks
plastered with mud for coolness.

In the house where the old man lived
the roofs were very high, with long-stalked ceiling-fans
growing down from them.

In that house
you walked from room to white-washed room
on deep, exquisite carpets
and the servants removed their shoes before entering.

The old man sat in his brick courtyard,
after all his sons had gone away
and the dust in the driveway rose in little puffs
when sprinkled with water of an evening.
He pulled at his cigarette through a clenched fist
and bemoaned the passage of time to the Deputy Commissioner.

SALMAN TARIK KURESHI

3

4

1. *Family portrait, Punjab.*
2. *Jeevni.*
3. *Mir Ahmed.*
4. *Shireen Bano.*
5. *Champa Bai.*
6. *Mohammed Ali.*
7. *Sain Ditto.*

6

7

97

Collecting firewood, Chitral, NWFP.

Grinding the golden hillside wheat to flour.

1. *Shalimar Gardens, Lahore, built by the Moghul emperor Shah Jehan in 1642.*
2. *Eid prayers at Badshahi Mosque, Lahore.*
3. *The Alamgiri Gate of the Lahore Fort, built by the emperor Aurangzeb in 1673–74.*
4. *Family going to the Eid prayers, Badshahi Mosque, Lahore.*
5. *Ranjit Singh's tomb glimpsed from the great courtyard of the Badshahi Mosque.*

1

2

3

(left) Carved window, Punjab.

*(above) The Shish Mahal, Palace of Mirrors, in Lahore.
In these pavilions, the emperor Jahangir is believed to have
dallied with a court dancer while still a prince.*

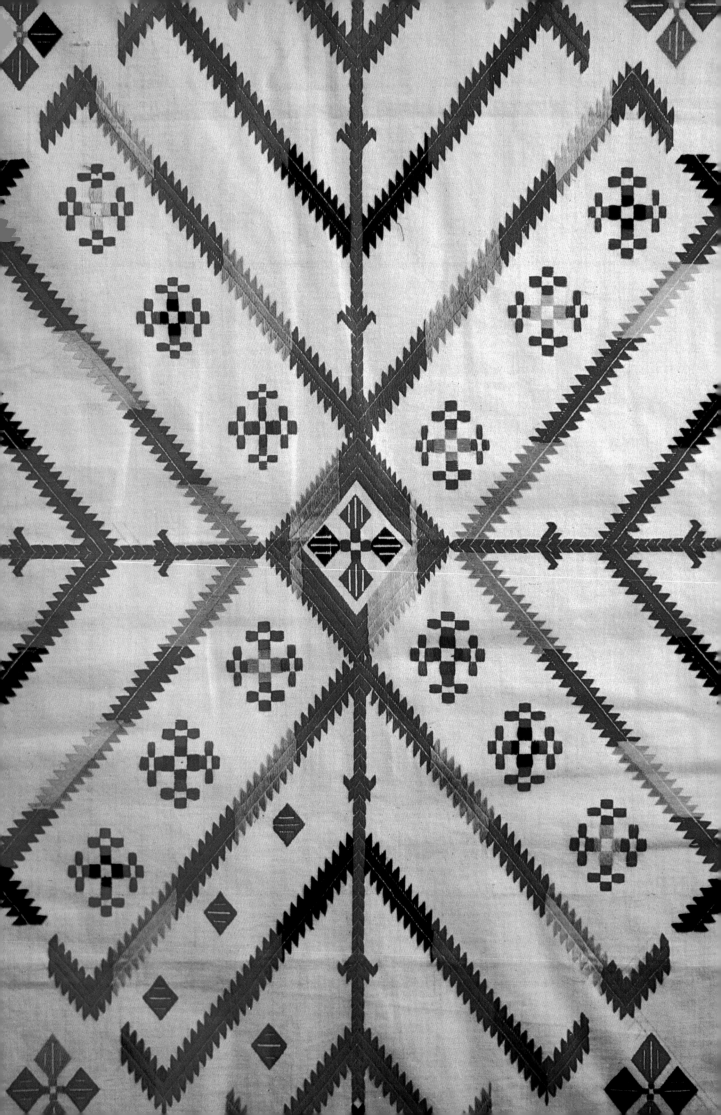

3 Patterns and Textures

The first time I remember seeing the Indus River, I was surprised that the water was brown, and not red, in color. It was a revelation to me. The year before—it was the year of the Partition riots—my *ayah* (governess) took me down to the canal that ran near our house in Lahore. It was evening, and the water was a brilliant red color. I thought it was a reflection of the sunset, but it was too homogeneous. "Why is the water red, Ama?" I asked my ayah. "It is the blood of the Indus," she said, "the whole country is bleeding to death."

FROM A TRANSCRIPT OF A RECOLLECTION OF THE 1947 EVENTS

The realities of climate and water that have formed the lives of Pakistanis are harsh. It is a geographically dramatic country—and the drama of the environment is the continuous ordeal of the inhabitants. Patterns of living are shaped and governed by external forces. Mud-plastered houses, sprinkled with a little water, are cool in summer; in winter the daytime sunshine warms them to meet the biting chill of nightfall. Deep verandas allow shelter and shade from the sun to those who can afford them.

History and economics have added their presence to nature. Fifty-five centuries of civilization—traditions and precedents molded into concrete realities over a hundred and seventy generations—are sometimes an immovable weight. The ever-deeper accumulations of silt, the residues of time, become an immobilizing blanket; their fecund richness becomes depleted and sterile. The consequence is poverty—a state where the act of survival itself absorbs so much human energy that there is little spirit left for exploring the quieter bylanes of life, that there is little put by, stored, or bequeathed to the future. History has been unkind in other ways as well. In 1947 political independence came to the land, and brought with it the trauma of the Partition riots. The nightmare began in late 1946, in Calcutta, capital of Bengal. For twelve days the city shook and shuddered as rival Hindu and Muslim mobs clashed. Suhrawardy, the Bengal chief minister, and Gandhi traveled the streets of Calcutta together to restore order and calm exploding passions. Many months afterward, they were still rehabilitating those whose homes had been burned and soothing the feelings of the mauled and bereaved. Hundreds had been killed and thousands rendered homeless.

The ferocity of the communal riots in Calcutta was only a portent of what was to follow. The inherent tensions between the two religious groups that had led inevitably to the now-imminent partition of the subcontinent had more than once exploded to riot. In Calcutta the true face of the specter—communal humiliation and hopeless deprivation finding release in raging nihilism—had been glimpsed. In response, the Muslim peasants of Noakhali (also in Bengal) went on the rampage against Hindu moneylenders and landlords. In the neighboring province of Bihar, Hindu mineworkers rioted in the towns. It took many weeks to restore order, and when Bengal and Bihar were quiet again, the city of Delhi simmered ominously. Armed troops were moved in. Lord Wavell was summoned to London by Prime Minister Attlee and informed that he was no longer Viceroy of India. Lord Mountbatten, the new viceroy, had left for Delhi while Wavell was still in the air. He had been commissioned to get the British out of India, and quickly. After a hundred and ninety years of colonial grandeur, more liberal sentiments had prevailed . . . or was it simply that the British wanted no part of the expected further violence?

April 1948 was fixed as the dateline for independence; Mountbatten had been given three hundred days. King George's cousin met with representatives of the Congress party, the Muslim League, the Sikh Akali Dal, the Scheduled Castes Federation, various Councils of Indian Princes, and other organizations. There were too many points of view, too many claims, too many brilliant lawyers on every side. In a fit of pique, Mountbatten shortened three hundred days to ninety. "We divide in August," he said.

The Muslims of the subcontinent rejoiced; Iqbal's Pakistan was being born. The Hindus celebrated separately. Then someone asked the "Punjab question." Sir Cyril Radcliffe, a British civil servant, drew some lines on a map, giving the communally near-balanced districts of Gurdaspur and Ferozepur to India. The Punjab question exploded to holocaust.

At first, there were sporadic skirmishes—fierce clashes between Hindu and Muslim, or Sikh and Muslim, militants. Then there were attacks on peoples' homes. New standards in violence were set, but this was only the beginning. As disorder raged, people began to leave their homes. The Muslims of East Punjab headed westward, and the Hindus and Sikhs of West Punjab went east. Fleeing families and groups of refugees were attacked. Thousands were killed or maimed; others were looted of their money and possessions; wives and daughters were molested, raped, or abducted. Special trains, each carrying many hundreds of refugees, began to run between the two newly independent countries.

And then came the day that a refugee train crossed the border, moving very slowly. It came to a stop signal, but kept on going. The switchman worked frantically to avert a collision. The train gradually lost speed, ran out of steam, and stopped. Those who ran to meet it stood looking through the carriage windows. Every man, woman, and child aboard had been murdered. No one was sure whether the first "train of the dead" carried Muslim refugees to Pakistan or Hindu and Sikh refugees to India. Whatever the truth, the nightmare had attained new dimensions. The reprisals on both sides escalated beyond the most horrifying predictions. There were many more such trains; the killing and looting became a geometrically multiplying series. Punjab was aflame.

In the wash of the Punjab bloodbath, communal disorders broke out in other cities, and refugees from all over were fleeing to and from Pakistan. The holocaust raged for many months. It would die down briefly and an uneasy calm would descend; then a fresh outrage would be committed by one side or the other, or news would come of an incident in some other part of the subcontinent, and the cannibal fires of hatred would burn again. It took many months and all the energies and efforts of seasoned public leaders to damp them down.

The people of Pakistan awoke from the nightmare of riots to the new reality of pestilence-stricken refugee camps. Five million people had arrived from East Punjab, jobless, homeless, penniless. Many were seriously injured or ill; others were in a state of shock from the brutalities and privations visited on them along the way, or from the slaughter of friends or family members. The reception centers on the Punjab borders and the camps in the towns and villages were grotesquely overcrowded. And now another 3 million refugees arrived from the UP, Rajasthan, Bombay, Bihar, and other parts of India.

About 12 million people had crossed both ways over the borders of what was then West Pakistan. Some four million moved in and out of East Bengal. It was the most massive movement of populations in human history. And over a million people had been murdered. In the years since, the refugees have found jobs or settled on farms or set up businesses. But the trauma of the events that accompanied independence lingers. It haunts the dreams of other Pakistanis as well; even those who were not themselves refugees were witness to the communal carnage in their towns and villages or had heard of what was happening elsewhere in the country. History and nature have dealt other blows to this land since. There have been floods, wars, riots, strikes, droughts, military coups, and epidemics. But the people have been able to take the worst with a certain equanimity, and even cynicism. After all, they had come through 1947.

THE TRUE COIN

The agonized genesis is perhaps what determines the Pakistani identity. In a land of such striking social and ethnic differences, so many varieties of consciousness, the dark bloodstain of 1947 is a common layer in each mind. The abstractions of the two-nation concept expounded and shaped by the founders of the country, the interactions and maneuvers of political leaders, the responses of followers—all materialized into the borders of the new nation. But ordinary life reemerges after the worst nightmare. The daily routine rechannels the panic of a shattered society. People go about their business and think of marriages and children, governments make decisions, and the small acts of living have their own impetus. In their homes and in their mosques, people offer quiet prayers to their Maker.

It is not surprising in a country whose very foundation is the principal religion of its people that the practice of religion is an important daily reality to almost every Pakistani. It is not that the Pakistani is an unusually fanatical or devout person; nor is his religion so ritualized that it occupies all his time. Religion is his simple explanation for the universe and for his own place in the scheme of things. Acts of devotion are part of his pattern of living, and the binding medium between himself and his community.

The Muslim faith split into two main sects very early in its history: the Sunni, centered in Arabia, and the Shiah, based in Persia. But many schools of Muslim thought have flourished over the centuries, and they have all found devotees and followers at some point. In a religion spread over many lands and peoples and not bound by an established Church, deviations from thought or practice that other faiths may have regarded as heretical have had a free hand. Over the centuries there has been a general crystallization at the two main poles of belief, and today most minor sects are really subsects of either the Shiah or the Sunni faiths. In Pakistan, as in most of the Muslim world, Sunnis outnumber Shiahs.

Within the broad framework of the faith, there is a wide variety in the actual modes of religious expression. Saintly adulation, for example, is a reality in shrine-centered pockets throughout Pakistan, but is most common in Sind and southern Punjab. It is sometimes elevated almost to the level of saint-worship and is accompanied by complex rituals and formulas. In the white-marble or blue-tiled serenity of a saintly tomb, as the inarticulable psychic peace of the environment descends, it is often hard to recall that saintly adulation has also had its ugly side. It seems out of place to remember how many descendants of saints have included oppressors, or how many childless couples prayed for a child at the tomb of Baba Bhullay Shah, only to give their first-born as a servant to the shrine.

Bhullay Shah would have been horrified at these practices once perpetrated in his name. He was a pungently witty poet in the Punjabi language, and was well known for his humanitarian views and actions. There was also a peculiarly impudent social radicalism in his intellectual makeup. A story goes that as a young man, he sat by the right hand of his *ustad* (teacher). A feast for the poor of the area had been prepared by a wealthy local, and Bhullay's ustad had been asked to give his blessing. "Bhullay," the ustad addressed his pupil, "distribute this food to the poor people outside." Bhullay asked, "Should it be distributed in the name of God or of the Prophet Mohammed (peace be on him)?" The ustad chided his pupil, "Mohammed (peace be on him) was only the Messenger of God; that is our faith. Distribute the food in the name of God, from Whom all good things flow."

Bhullay divided the feast into four equal parts. The first two parts he placed before the wealthy patron; the third part he placed before the ustad. The fourth part he divided in half; keeping one half for himself, he began to distribute the meager remainder to the several hundred needy people waiting outside. "But what are you doing?" exclaimed the ustad. "What is this blasphemy?" Bhullay answered: "The Prophet Mohammed (peace be on him) was a man and understood the needs of men. He would have given equally to all, or more to those that needed most. But God? Well, His ways are inscrutable. He has made the world as it is, and the good things which flow from Him seem to come in just such proportions." It is not recorded whether Bhullay's ustad was enraged or enlightened by this observation of his great pupil.

Outside the market village of Khudian Khas near Lahore, a large signboard was put up by the officials of the birth-control program. The board was divided down the center into two pictures: The one on the left showed a smiling man and woman with two well-dressed children; the one on the right showed a brood of seven bony brats, presided over by a harried, ill-dressed man and his frantic wife. The implications were clear, thought the authors of the program, even if the local farmers could not read the writing under the pictures. But the farmers looked at the signboard and walked away, clucking their tongues in sympathy for the man on the left. "Poor fellow," they said, "he only has two children."

City intellectuals discussed the birth-control program and explained to each other why it had seemingly failed. "It is linked with a virility complex," they said; "a man is not believed to be a man if he has no children." Others said, "Actually, the blame lies in our medieval attitudes to religion. The *maulvis* (priests) do not have a sufficiently modern outlook." As evidence, they pointed to the fulminations against the ungodly institution of contraception issuing from pulpits around the land. A lady social worker visiting the village of Pakka Anna (the name means "true coin") received an unusually frank opinion from a man she spoke with. "You come from the city," she was told. "Your sari is clean; you must have many saris. You came in a motor car. You are very different from us . . . and yet you tell us it is for our good not to have children. When you grow old, you will have someone to look after you; perhaps the government. When I grow old and cannot work, all I will have are my family, my children, and my grandchildren." Economics, and not religion, is the barrier to change in this, as in many other things. The village maulvi who agitated against the family planning program comprehended this social reality better than the educated city woman. He also understood psychology when he translated economic insecurity into male pride and produced scripture and verse as justification.

The maulvi of Pakka Anna was a middle-aged man grown somewhat embittered with life. His name was Abdul Hakim; he belonged to the village and had spent most of his years ministering to the religious needs of his parishioners. In the dusty courtyard of the mosque, he had taught their children to read and write a few words and to do arithmetic. He had instructed young minds in the meaning of the Koran and taught them their prayers. He had taught them how, and how often, to wash themselves and how to order their lives. It pained him to see how few followed these precepts when they grew to adulthood. One of his favorite former pupils, now a teenager, had been forced to leave the village because he had been caught by the canal with two different girls in successive weeks; a third girl had announced herself pregnant by him. With three families after him, this young rakehell had thought it wiser to seek his fortune elsewhere. Such incidents, and their predictable frequency, pained Maulvi Hakim.

Recently the government had opened a primary school in Pakka Anna. The maulvi did not resent this, because the school did not teach many of the things he could teach, and the children still came to him for religious and other instruction. But he did resent the lack of recognition for the labor of half a lifetime and a prematurely graying beard. During the last elections, he had agitated (on the instructions of the party to whose program he subscribed) against liberals and socialists. "Islam is in danger," he had thundered. But the villagers had voted solidly against his party. Maulvi Hakim was convinced that the Day of Judgment must be at hand. The times were out of joint; anarchy was being unleashed on the world. But despite all, he would patiently continue performing what he considered his duty in the eyes of God.

A maulvi is not a formal priest; there is no ordained priesthood in Islam. Maulvis are lay religious instructors who preside at ceremonies and impart the meaning of the scriptures to believers. The Muslim maulvi is similar to the Jewish rabbi in his function and position in society; the formal priestly classes of Catholicism and orthodox Christianity would seem to be products of European, not Semitic, traditions. Among Pakistani maulvis, there are many schools of thought and many tendencies. Even in their political views, they are far from unified; there are maulvis who belong to or vote for socialist parties, liberal parties, centrist parties, and conservative parties. In fact, most parties vie for the support of members of the *ulama* (as the group of religious leaders is known), since few other community figures have the opportunity of addressing a congregation every Friday to expound on their ideas. Inevitably, though, the dominant social views of maulvis tend to conservatism, and they play the role of keepers of the traditional verities and virtues.

Although the status of a maulvi seems to depend on his individual efforts, it is also conditioned by the social framework of each region. He is certainly always an important formative influence on religious attitudes. In the countryside particularly, he is likely to be one of the few educated men in each village, and his views on more secular matters may also carry weight. As an arbiter of day to day conduct, however, his role is minimal. The universal needs of the body and the psyche; the realities of making a living and getting on with people; the normal human impulses, desires, and aspirations—all these are far more important determinants of human behavior and attitudes than the words of a religious instructor, however respected he may be as a person, and however deep-rooted the religion among the members of a community.

THE VEIL

The word *purdah* means "curtain," and Muslim women are enjoined to draw a "curtain of modesty" around themselves. The concept bears little relevance to the clothes a woman may or may not wear; in fact, Pakistani clothes, in their figure-molding looseness, are scarcely unflattering to the women who wear them. The concept of "purdah" really refers to public behavior. "The secret of modesty is in the eyes," an aging lady told her grandniece. "Guard your eyes. When visitors come, smile your smile of welcome to them; but drop your eyes immediately afterward, so that your smile may not be construed as an unchaste invitation."

The all-covering garment that a few women wear—the enveloping *burkah* through which only the eyes of the wearer are visible—is not an imperative. The burkah is a device not so much of modesty as of anonymity. The eyes may tell whatever tale they like, may stare unabashedly into the eyes of a stranger; the hands may beckon in invitation, or brush past in a fleeting caress. The identity of the burkah-clad woman will remain concealed, the invitation merely a meaningless flirtation. But this is not the "purdah" of modesty enjoined on women. There are, in any case, very few burkahs in Pakistan. It is not so much that wearing these garments is a dying practice, but simply that it has never been widespread. Nor is the Pakistani burkah a local variant of the North African *yashmaq;* its derivation is quite different. In ancient times, the ladies of noble Hindu households ventured out of their homes only in palanquins carried by loyal servants. The purpose was to spare them the effort of walking. The casual clothing of the times, worn at home, was very scanty; while it was considered perfectly proper in the presence of family members, it would be wrong to permit lower-caste men in the marketplace to admire the bodies of princesses. Proper "public" clothing, in the hot climate, could be uncomfortable. So these ladies rode, in comfortable near-nudity, inside their heavily curtained *palkis.*

For the aristocratic households of the later Muslim rulers of northern India—the Afghans, Persians, Turks, and Moghuls—the palki became a status symbol; wives and daughters of the nobility simply did not appear in public, except in palkis. But this proved awkward, and before long such ladies began to carry their palanquins with them in the form of long garments that covered them from head to ankle. The burkah had been invented. The families of urban courtiers and scribes and others close to the nobility copied this garment from their masters, as much to conceal their wives from a wandering noble eye as for any other reason. In modern times, when most of the wealthier families had shed the burkah, it lingered—and still lingers—in many middle-class, white-collar households, though it is dying even among them. Some feel this is a sign of "emancipation." Even if it is, it is not a significant sign, for "emancipation" is not a strong force among Pakistani women. Emancipation is a state of mind; a liberation crusade requires something to be liberated from, a tangible institution that opposes the advancement or interests of a group.

In Western societies, where economic advancement has offered significant job opportunities, sexually discriminatory employment practices are just such a target. So since the early part of the present century, Western women have fought for political rights and the repeal of discriminatory laws and statutes. In Pakistan, political rights were achieved by women at the same time as men. Muslim customary law gave women a position unusual among societies at the time of its codification. As the law expanded through judicial interpretation over the centuries, the only areas of discrimination that survived into modern times were the customs relating to divorce and polygamy, and these were amended by legislation. Nor is there significant job discrimination. Pakistani society has traditionally accepted women teachers, lawyers, doctors, social workers, and even engineers and accountants. In 1964, when Fatima Jinnah ran for the Presidency of Pakistan, the fact of her being a woman drew less comment than John Kennedy's Catholicism did in the America of 1960. It was not considered in any way unusual that a woman should run for the highest office in the land.

In the villages, a woman is expected to carry a workload equal to her husband's; at home she is the decision-maker, and in the fields she is a helpmate. In the towns and elsewhere, women have long been construction laborers. They are not, however, found in the skilled trades; female labor tends to be casual labor. The needs of childbearing and rearing have not given women the "freedom" to acquire the skills necessary for careers as mechanics or welders. Nevertheless, the head of the Karachi Shipyard Workers Union is a woman. Women work as a rule in Pakistan because most families are poor and can use extra money. But their labor is divided between the roles of being a money-earner and being, simply, a woman. Economic necessity has amended the essential concept of femininity, a concept deep-rooted in the Pakistani consciousness.

Women are feminine, and anything that hinders the expression of this femininity is bad. There is a double standard, certainly, a separate code of behavior for each sex. It is a double standard that says the two sexes are different; not superior and inferior, just different. In this conceptual context, it is in the woman's being that the dark mysteries of life are enacted. Men merely arrange and administer the outside world. It is the woman who is the creator and mistress of that most fundamental of all Asian institutions—the home. It is the woman who is the repository of all that is beautiful or graceful in life.

In the old days, young scions of lordly households were sent to courtesans when they grew to puberty not to gain sexual experience (it was assumed they could find adequate means of their own), but to complete their educations. They were taught music and poetry and good manners; they were taught the cultivated responses of a gentleman. It was assumed that only a woman could instill a consciousness of the higher, finer values. Although the education of courtly noblemen is a far pole from the tasks of a country housewife in a mud-plastered cottage, the same essential concept governs her life. She is, in a word and in all its implications, feminine. It is a double standard; but the Pakistani woman's confident pride in her female role can make the slogans of women's liberationists seem like gratuitous self-indulgence, far removed from the fulfillment, the grace, and the harshness of Asian reality.

A QUESTION OF MORALITY

The Muslim religion, like most others, has its puritanical manifestations. But in Pakistan at least, the more rigid interpretations of moral codes are seldom encountered outside the cities, and even in the cities they are a middle-class luxury. In the countryside, attitudes toward sexual morality are surprisingly tolerant. Premarital sex, for example, is not condoned, but it is accepted as a reality that suggests its own solution: early marriage. The concomitants are not infrequent lapses in marital fidelity and a high divorce rate. Most people tend to accept these as realities of life. However strict the moral code, the fact remains that human beings have passions and emotions, and these are often irrational, or even immoral.

The permissive realism of the country folk is not always shared by city people. Urban values are governed by the bourgeoisie, and, like others of their class in other parts of the world, they have their share of middle-class morality. The Pathans of the northwest also tend to take a dimmer view of sexual laxity than the people of the plains. Pathan social relations are patriarchal and chivalrous. They are governed by the *rawaj*, or tribal customary law, and conditioned by the concept of *pakhtoonwali* (Pathan honor). A Pathan's *wali* must always be vindicated, even if he breaks the law to do it. And he may invoke any of the four principles of pakhtoonwali on other Pathans: *melmastia*, the ritual of hospitality, to be extended even to an enemy who has invoked it; *nanawati*, the law of asylum; *badragga*, the right of safe conduct; and *badal*, the right to vengeance. Such an honor-conscious ethical framework has its own romantic appeal, but it is sternly intolerant of moral lapses, which it sees in terms of the slighted honor of a man, a family, or a tribe. And an insult to honor is unpardonable.

Personal honor and pride are potent motives for all Pakistanis, though not always so stern or systematic as in the northern mountains. There are also many questions of morality that have consistently defied easy value judgments. One such is the institution of polygamy, which is nowhere near as common as it is believed to be, but is a living reality for some. Polygamy is permitted under Muslim customary law, but heavily hedged about by conditions and qualifications. It is discouraged and rendered near-impossible by Pakistani amendments to the customary law, but it still occurs. Nor is it always feasible for legislation and legal processes to provide solutions for what is essentially a human problem.

In the hills of central Baluchistan lived a small tribe, a sept of the Zarakzai clan. Their village was an itinerant settlement that changed its location from season to season, following the never-ending peregrinations of their sheep and goats. In the ambulatory village lived a herdsman named Qadir Bux, who numbered among his offspring a sixteen-year-old daughter called Fatima. Fatima became friendly with a young man from the village. He brought her presents—a jar of honey, bangles, flowers—and she often sneaked away from her family duties for long walks into the hills with him. One day her brothers followed the couple. They returned leading the now-battered young man at dagger-point, their weeping sister following behind. They took him before Qadir Bux. "This young man has outraged our sister's virtue." It was decided that a marriage should be contracted immediately, and the young man was ordered to go to his family and bring a formal proposal. To everyone's astonishment, Fatima interceded, saying, "But I do not *want* to marry him." Qadir Bux asked her why, and she said, "He is a shiftless loafer. He is not the kind of man you would have chosen for me, father. I leave the choice to you . . . but let it be someone else."

Much argument ensued, but Fatima remained insistent that she must be allowed to fulfill the duties of a daughter. So the bewildered young man was sent home, and cautioned to silence lest the matter should come before the tribal jirga. The next day Qadir Bux sent for the village matchmaker and explained his requirements in a son-in-law. The aging woman told him of one Rahimdad Khan, who was from their tribe. This young man had gone away to work for a mining company near Kalat; he had done well for himself and was now a foreman. He had recently written to the matchmaker to find him a wife from his own tribe. Qadir Bux felt he sounded all right; the matchmaker informed Rahimdad's parents in the village and also wrote him a letter in Kalat. Rahimdad's father came to see Qadir Bux, bringing with him a basket of fruits, a sheepskin rug, and a wash-and-wear shirt (made in Hong Kong) which his son had sent him. Matters were discussed, details explained and sorted out, a date set.

Rahimdad arrived two months later. He was tall, handsome, and bore all the marks of his well-earned success. After the marriage, he and Fatima lived a month at his parents' home in the village, and then left for Kalat. At the end of the long, dusty journey—by camel, by bus, and on foot—Fatima entered her new home, a small stone house on the outskirts of a mineworkers' colony. Her tired elation turned to stark dismay when Rahimdad introduced her to his two other wives.

Fatima did not know what to do. At the first opportunity, she went to the local scribe and dictated a letter to her father explaining her predicament and asking for advice. The reply came many weeks later. Qadir Bux said he had known all along that Rahimdad was already married; but, since he was a fine man, he had not objected. He expected his daughter to adjust to the situation; after all, adjustment was required of any girl when she went to her new home. However, he wrote, if the situation was absolutely impossible, he would accept her home again.

It was intolerable. The three women slept in separate beds in the one large room, one or the other of them being invited to share the night with their husband in his adjoining bedroom. This privilege was enjoyed by Fatima for the first few nights, and each morning when she returned she was greeted with the jibes and taunts of the other two women. There were also two little children, who slept in a separate room. The first few days had been the worst, with both the elder wives teamed up against her. But then Reshma, the eldest wife, had softened, and she and Fatima had become friends. Sohagan, the second wife, now fought with both of them.

Bit by bit, Fatima pieced together the story of her husband's three marriages. He had married Reshma, a Kalat girl, five years back, shortly after he had come to work here. Rahimdad's second marriage had occurred a year ago, when his best friend was killed in a mining accident. The widow, Sohagan, had no family to return to, so he had married her to give her a home. Rahimdad had felt all along that it was only proper he have a wife from his own tribe, and that was how Fatima had come to join his household.

The politics of this multiple home were incredibly complex. Sohagan was angered at Reshma's friendship with Fatima, and frequently turned her wrath on both of them. Just as often, though, the two older women leveled a joint attack on Fatima. The two children (who were both Reshma's) did not like Fatima. They ran away whenever she approached; or they stood there, staring at her out of large, frightened eyes, the boy clinging to the older girl. To make matters worse, Sohagan was in an advanced state of pregnancy. This meant she was excluded from household chores and lay in bed while the other wives ministered to her. Whenever this galling duty fell to Fatima, she was greeted by a volley of abuse from the pregnant woman. Being quick-tempered herself, she often responded vituperatively.

Rahimdad was continually being called in to mediate the three-cornered quarrels. One of the bitterest had occurred the day after Reshma had spent the night in her husband's room, the first time this had happened since Fatima's arrival. Fatima wept bitterly all night. The next day, when Reshma asked her to fill a pot of water, Fatima threw the vessel at the older girl. Sohagan laughed loudly from her bed, and Reshma turned on both of them. The cacophany of their three voices was audible to the whole neighborhood when Rahimdad returned for his midday meal. Throwing up his hands in despair, he stalked out of the house. He did not return that night, nor the next day. A worried hush fell on his three wives. They must find out where he had gone. Reshma would go. No, said Fatima, she would go. And a fresh quarrel broke out, to be silenced by Sohagan suggesting that Reshma's daughter should go. Rahimdad, located at the home of another foreman, sent word that he would come home only if his wives stopped quarreling. So a truce was declared and Rahimdad returned.

Fatima bore with the tension and the intermittent quarrels as the weeks passed. The worst was the gnawing, enervating jealousy when any attention was paid to another wife. Since Rahimdad was fairly even-handed with his affections, this meant two-thirds of the time. And then Qadir Bux's letter arrived. Fatima decided to sell some of her bridal jewelry and use the money to return home. But not immediately. She would be needed in the household until Sohagan's child was born.

Sohagan, who bore Rahimdad a daughter, fell very ill with childbed fever, and so Fatima was required to nurse her baby. By the time the mother was better, Fatima discovered that she was pregnant herself. She could not leave. Sohagan was more friendly toward Fatima now, and she would bring her an occasional glass of *lassi* (sweetened whey) or a bowl of curds. But one night Fatima discovered an unusual object under her pillow. It was a tiny figurine made from sticks and wax, with a lock of hair very much like Fatima's own on its head. She showed it to Reshma, who said, "It is a *totkha* (hex symbol). Sohagan is trying black magic on you now." Sohagan, when confronted, insisted that it must be Reshma.

Fatima was bewildered and frightened. Everything about her seemed to be an omen of evil. The dark shadow of a high-flying hawk fell on her as she looked out of the window one day. Another time, a goat came up to her outside the house and seemed to stare at her strangely. One evening she spilled some milk, and she could have sworn that it rose out of the bowl. As she stood there, paralyzed with fear, Rahimdad arrived. She told him of the nameless, ancient evil that was being raised against her. He scoffed at the idea. "There is no such thing as witchcraft," he said. Fatima went to the maulvi. He also said, "There is no such thing." To reassure her, he gave her an amulet containing a verse from the Koran. Fatima now felt more confident. Nothing could harm her with the words of God upon her person. The only time she removed it was when she bathed.

The daily bath was a communal affair for the women. At midmorning, they would make a four-sided barricade of rope cots in the small walled courtyard in front of their house. While one wife squatted on the ground, another would pour water over her, and the third would soap her body (soap was one of the luxuries their husband's position provided) and scrub hard with a flat piece of pumice stone. Afterward they would take turns combing and braiding one another's long hair. On one occasion, they were dressing again when Fatima found her amulet missing. They searched together, but it could not be found.

Fatima was sick with fear. Without her amulet, she was defenseless against witchcraft—whatever her husband and the maulvi might say. A few days later, to complete her nightmare, she found another totkha. Then the spell of the totkhas seemingly began to work. Fatima fell seriously ill with a high fever and agonizing body pains. The local *hakim* (medical man) who examined her could find nothing wrong. "It is as if she were bewitched," he said. Fatima heard this and became hysterical. Rahimdad stalked out of the house and walked eleven miles to the mining company's head office for a proper doctor. The doctor too could find nothing wrong. Her condition worsened until one day, as if by a miracle, her amulet was found again—under her pillow. Within a day the fever was gone; within a week she was up and about again.

When Fatima's son was born, her husband was overjoyed. She, however, again began to think about returning to her parents. Although the overt tensions of her multiple household were much less in evidence now, nothing could take away the intolerable pangs of jealousy, the dreadful fact of having to share the love of a man with two others. And she, as the third wife, had received the least portion of love. But what were the alternatives? In her own way, she cared deeply for Rahimdad, cared far more than she had for anyone. Even if she were to go home again and seek a divorce (leaving her son with his two stepmothers), she could not live with her parents indefinitely. Who would marry her, with the stigma of divorce on her? And, worse, the humiliation of having been a third wife. No, her options were too limited. She would have to resign herself to her situation and accept her life as it was.

Fatima remained Rahimdad's third wife, snatching what little share of love came her way from time to time, fighting for the rights of her son (and the children she later had) against those of the children of the other two wives. She sometimes felt a swollen bitterness at her fate, but she never once questioned the moral right of a man to have three wives. It was, after all, not a question of morality. It was a question of her circumstances, her fate.

THE LAND-BOUND

Tribal society, for all its rigid ethical codes, is bound to the land. It is the land— enriched by the waters of rivers, canals, or wells—that feeds their flocks and rears their children. It is also the land that binds the farmers, artisans, and merchants of the nontribal societies of the plains. Even when they migrate to the cities in search of jobs, the contact with the land is maintained through their families or kinfolk. A city-born Pakistani, when asked where he "belongs," will name the village from which his father or grandfather came, and where his country cousins still live. The land-bound ones—the townfolk, the farmers, the herdsmen—are the ancient ordinary heart of this young country. Most of them are poor, by objective standards; but objective standards can be misleading. Poverty may be a quantifiable fact, but the response to it is certainly relative. Pakistanis who travel abroad are likely to find the slums of London or the ghettos of New York far more dramatically distressing than the slums of Karachi; and the Karachi slums, in their turn, more startling than the generalized poverty of Pakistani villages.

It is not merely that poverty in the industrialized West is the more stark because of the contrast with the surrounding affluence; the Asian gulf between the rich and the not-rich is far more striking than the European. It is that the deprived person in Europe is just that: deprived. He lacks something—a television set, a car, or whatever—that another man, a man who is substantially the same as he, has. In a country like Pakistan, the situation is reversed. It is not so much that the poor lack something, as that the rich have something additional which the not-rich perhaps do not even want. Each ethnic or religious community has its own life style; so does each economic group. Each wears different clothing, frequently speaks different languages, and has differing standards and aspirations.

The servant of an affluent home was asked, "You handle expensive objects all day long; are you not tempted to steal?" He looked amazed, and then replied: "These things belong to the owner of this estate, but I am part of them. They brought me up, I live here among them. They would do anything for me I should ask. Why would I risk my present comfort, home, and family, for a mean theft?" A serving girl reacted to this strange query by saying: "Yes, my employers have a lovely home and many beautiful things . . . but look how unhappy they are! I would not exchange my life for the pain and responsibility which seems to come along with beautiful clothes, jewelry, and fancy houses."

The life styles of these differing communities seem neither to correspond nor to conflict; and the life style of poverty is a distinctive reality. It too has its own philosophy, its own manner. The very institutions of daily life have grown out of what can be found available. Meat, for example, is expensive on the plains and few can afford it, so it is seldom eaten. The need for protein is satisfied by lentils, prepared in hundreds of ways, and by many ways of drinking milk. Because a diet of vegetables may prove bland, pungent mustard oil is used for cooking, and mustard leaves chopped up like spinach are made into a curry to be eaten with corn bread fried around chopped horseradish. Wood is scarce, and coal is expensive. So, for many centuries the ordinary fuel has been dried cow dung. The moisture of the drying cakes plastered on the outside walls cools the inside of the house; the ashes after burning are mixed with leaf mold for the fields.

At its sociological level, poverty in a pre-industrial society means a society dispersed into many units of varying size—family, village, clan. The homogenizing influences of industrialization are marginal; localized ethnic and cultural institutions have remained intact. Thus, the uniquely hued variety of a country like Pakistan, the many-faceted texture that covers an identical pulse.

At the junction between past and future, the attempt is to carry the entire accumulation of the wealth of the past intact into the striven-for future of plenty. The ideal is to conserve the richness found even, or most of all, in an environment of poverty. For poverty, in this context, does not imply deprivation. It has its own fulfillments, its own satisfactions and rewards, its own imperatives and standards. It says, in effect, "This is life, and life is hard. But life can be made beautiful." A television set may be too expensive; but everyone can afford some beauty. It is found in little things, in small, perfect details. It is seen in clothing, in the vanities of personal appearance, in small items of daily use adorned with colored threads and beads; it is hung about the walls of grimy huts.

It is the beauty of a simplicity that owes nothing to the sophistications of graphic designers. It is the beauty of tradition and custom wedded to a millenniums-old pattern of life. It is the beauty of sudden, dazzling displays—the color riots of the Eid festivals and marriages. It is the beauty of Basant Bahar, the Festival of Spring, when the skies turn to a paper-hung fantasy of kites of every color, kites that wheel and dip and swerve at the end of long, arched strings reaching down to ecstatic brown children. It is the beauty nurtured and cherished and developed in the human responses of people. It is life, and its flamboyant celebration, in the regions drained and watered by the Indus.

STRANDS

But all the land-bound do not know the quieter fulfillments of life. There are those whose lives are replete with drama and desperation and pride. In the barren eastern reaches of the province of Sind live the Hurs, the "free ones"— proud, independent desert nomads who follow the individual known as the pir (saint) of Pagaro. In July 1942, when the British army was locked in the worldwide war against the Fascist Axis, a Hur named Sain Rakhio Bihan walked down to the sweet-water well that fed the tiny oasis in which he lived. It was a hard, dry desert day, and the Loo, the hot wind that blows west from Indian Rajasthan, was kicking up eddies in the sands. Sain Rakhio needed water to sprinkle on the rush-covered floor of his cottage. He wiped the penetrating sand from his brow and looked up, squinting at the blurred glare of the sun. An amazing sight met his eyes. There, high in the transparent sky, huge white flowers had blossomed. He blinked and looked again. They were still there, and they were floating slowly downward. Sain Rakhio ran back to his cottage and called to his wife, Mai Mithi. "Look," he said, "look up. Am I seeing things?" But Mai Mithi also saw the flowers. As they sank nearer the earth, she pointed out that the white blossoms had dark stalks—dark, man-shaped stalks. Suddenly Rakhio understood. Newspaper reports of the world war had been read to him, and he had heard stories and seen photographs of paratroopers—gunmen who dropped suddenly from the sky. Quickly, Rakhio saddled his best camel, took a sword and a gun, and rode into the desert with his wife. He rode like a madman for many sandy miles until he reached the village of Pirjo Goth (Village of the Saint). He strode into the cottage of Mohbat Fakir, one of the leaders of the Hur rebellion, and announced: "The British are attacking with paratroops now."

The events leading up to this particular moment had begun many centuries before. Sindhi society in medieval times had tended to neglect the desert wanderers, the itinerant nomads of the barren reaches in the east of the region. A man known to history and legend as the first pir of Pagaro, the shadowy ancestor of the present pir, had gone among these nomads. He had converted them to the Muslim faith and helped them set up civic and social institutions. "You are the Hurs," he had told them, "the free ones. And, as free men, you have come to the God of Islam."

Around 1815, the pir of that time grew wary of the British presence hovering about the borders of Sind. He feared that the Muslim faith was in danger; even if the white infidels did not seek actual domination of Sind, there could be a dilution of the native culture and beliefs. The Hurs must organize themselves for defense against the aliens. The peaceful flock, the nonmilitant majority of Hurs, would be guarded by a small band of so-called Fakirs hand-picked from time to time by the pir himself. Pledged to sacrifice life, property, and family in the defense of their cause, the Hur Fakirs were a permanent death squad, the shock troops of the pir of Pagaro. Against any outside attacker, they had the unique advantage of total familiarity with the harsh desert country in which they lived.

The British "dealt" with the Hur guerrilla bands by the simple expedient of staying out of their territories; the hegemony of the Raj spread over Sind without coming into conflict with the Hurs. Treaties were eventually negotiated, and the Hurs remained neutral during the upheavals of 1857. In the 1880s a Hur rebellion erupted. The Fakirs of the pir of Pagaro spread themselves in pockets over an area very much larger than they had previously occupied. Perhaps they had spread themselves too thin. Intermittent fighting continued for years, but the Hurs made no significant dent in the well-diffused pattern of British authority. The pir concluded another treaty with the Raj, and the rebellion was over.

In the 1930s, a young incumbent pir of Pagaro, Pir Sabghatullah Shah, was arrested by the Raj under the Preventive Detention Laws. The British feared the potential menace of the commander of the Hur Fakirs at a time of nationalist disorder in the subcontinent. They thought a few stints in prison would teach the young pir an object lesson before any rebellious thoughts entered his head. But they were wrong. In the prisons of the time, which came to be known as "nationalist training schools," Pir Sabghatullah came in contact with people whose ideas changed his outlook. His feudal insularity was transformed into anticolonial fervor, and he emerged from prison with a specific program of action in mind.

Pir Sabghatullah was unconvinced by the "nonviolent" program that Gandhi had imposed on the Congress party, and he could not see the Muslim League's constitutionalist approach leading to the expulsion of the British. In this, of course, he was mistaken; but he was a believer in action. Over the years, he planned the tactics of the guerrilla campaign he proposed. He drilled his Fakirs in the techniques of desert survival and the sudden, unexpected blow at the enemy. World War II was a godsend for this nascent terrorist: British energies, arms, and attention were involved with the Germans in Europe and Africa and the Japanese in Asia. One of the secret caches of arms Pir Sabghatullah had begun to amass for his men was discovered by British Intelligence. The pir was arrested in October 1941, tried, and sentenced to death. As he languished in prison, the Hur rebellion broke out.

Although they were leaderless, each Hur knew his part, for the details of the campaign had been meticulously planned. It began with the cutting of the telegraph and telephone wires that ran through the desert and the mining of selected points on the roads. Then there were sudden hit-and-run attacks on police outposts and isolated military garrisons. Each time, the Hur attackers melted away into the desert before the troops of the authorities could find them. In March 1942, the Sind Legislative Assembly passed the Hur Act, empowering the government to take any action necessary to quell the revolt. Hur farmers and others whose relatives were militant Fakirs were arrested and held hostage. The response of the Fakirs was a bold daylight attack on the Lahore Mail Express train. The authorities placed Sind under martial law. British paratroops were airdropped near Hur strongholds. Tanks prowled the desert, razing the Hur villages they came upon. The Royal Air Force was brought in for strafing attacks and bombing raids on Hur settlements. In March 1943, Pir Sabghatullah was executed, but the rebellion continued.

The next few years were ones of fierce guerrilla resistance. General Richardson deployed an entire regiment in Sind, at a time when the war in Burma was at its height and Rommel was operating in Africa. Internment camps were set up, and the inhabitants of entire Hur villages were imprisoned. The fighting was still going on in 1947, when the Hurs at last surrendered their arms to the government of their newly created country of Pakistan. In the years since, many of the "free ones" have turned to farming. They are a proud, prickly people, and the more oppressive feudal landlords find Hur tenants hard to keep down. A landowner in Upper Sind forced his attentions on the daughter of one of his tenants, who happened to be a Hur. That night his house was surrounded by Hur Fakirs, who seemed to appear from nowhere, and his dead body was found the next morning. There has been no arrest or conviction so far, and the case is filed under "unsolved crimes" in the registers of the local police.

In the rigidly racial structure of Raj authority, the children of occasional unions between native women and Englishmen were anomalous. Their in-between status brought them education in schools that taught in English and jobs in the lower echelons of government and corporate officialdom. Their descendants are the Anglo-Indians, the small Eurasian community of Pakistan and India.

Anglo-Indians speak English with a distinctive accent identifiable anywhere in the subcontinent. In independent Pakistan, they constitute an educated, if ingrown, community. They are frequently employed in executive and supervisory positions in the railways and the police and as schoolteachers; they often complain of discriminatory promotions, while their detractors accuse them of inwardness and unreliability. The community is small in numbers and slowly dwindling as younger Anglo-Indians emigrate to England or Canada. Their tightly closed pattern of values has caused them to become sadly isolated from the society in which they live. A traditional exclusivism that helped generate suspicion and antipathy has further hardened the Anglo-Indian's chosen isolation, although there are many notable exceptions to this observation.

Anglo-Indians constitute a small minority of the 2 million Pakistani Christians, who are a different group, though the two communities sometimes overlap socially. Pakistani Christians are the descendants of native converts, principally from Hinduism, but they are divided culturally into two classes. The educated products of the missionary-run schools and colleges parallel Anglo-Indians in that they are English-speaking and pursue similar occupations. There is a great deal of intercourse between the Anglo-Indian community and educated Pakistani Christians; but the latter, being a very much larger community, are less insular and exclusive. Many of them come originally from Goa (until recently a Portuguese enclave on the South Indian coast), and they sport Portuguese surnames and Anglicized first names. So do many other Pakistani Christians not specifically of Goan origin—tribute to the activities of Portuguese missionaries, and the esteem in which the order of St. Ignatius Loyola and St. Francis Xavier is held among subcontinental Christians. Goans are an elite among Pakistani Christians, and live mainly in Karachi and Lahore. The native Goan language, Konkinese (a Tamil offshoot), is now spoken by only a very few elderly people in Karachi.

The broad mass of Pakistani Christians, however, do not have the benefit of Portuguese surnames or missionary-school educations. Some of them still pursue the hereditary occupations of the Hindu caste from which they sought escape through conversion; they are sweepers, offal-carriers, bathroom-washers, and gravediggers. They do not speak English, although their church services are often conducted in that language.

In the legal parlance of the land, non-Muslim peoples are known as the "minority communities." Apart from Christians, who are scattered throughout the country, there are Hindus (mainly in Sind), some few Buddhists, the occasional Sikhs, and the Parsees. There are only a few thousand Parsees, living mainly in Karachi, but they are an exceptionally visible community. There is a saying among older residents of Karachi to the effect that "most Parsees are millionaires, and those who are not are embarrassed to admit that they are billionaires."

In their small white temples, Parsee ladies and gentlemen worship their sacred eternal flame. Theirs is an ancient religion; it is the creed preached by the great Zoroaster among the Aryans of Persia during the days of the Persian Empire. The golden emperors—Darius and Cyrus—adored the same sacred flame, the light of God Incarnate, as do the Parsees of Karachi. Christianity came to Persia in the third century A.D. and made many converts from Zoroastrianism. When Islam swept the Aryan lands in the sixth and seventh centuries, Zoroastrians became a rapidly dwindling minority, and by the twelfth century, the ancient creed was almost extinct. A small group of believers left Iran and established themselves as traders on the Gujarat coast of India, particularly at the port of Bombay.

Parsees (the name is derived from Farsi, or Persian; later Zoroastrian immigrants from Persia call themselves Iranis) have for centuries married only within their own community. Those who strayed outside were excommunicated. Their numbers have dwindled further over the generations as attrition, in-breeding, and occasional conversions and excommunications have taken their toll. In Pakistan, all Parsees speak Gujrati, the language of Bombay. They are the old-time gentry, the "leading citizens" of Karachi. They came over to the budding port town in the eighteenth and nineteenth centuries as traders, merchants, and shipbuilders. The wealth they amassed contributed to the building of the city, and of the country of which it became part.

MUJIBULLAH KHAN'S BIO-DATA

A Karachi-based manufacturer of soaps and cheap cosmetics had advertised for a salesman. The personnel manager of the company waded through more than two hundred applications. One of them was on embossed notepaper, with a crest in the upper left-hand corner; the address was that of a shabbily genteel middle-class neighborhood in Karachi. The bio-data enclosed with the application read:

Full name:	Major Nawabzada Mujibullah Khan
Father's name:	His Highness, the late Nawab Sir Mohammed Ibrahim Khan, Maharajah of D—— (a princely state in central India).
Date of birth:	3rd September 1918.
Place of birth:	D——.
Educated at:	St. Xavier's High School, Bombay; Royal Indian Military Academy, Dehra Dun.
Professional experience:	1. After passing out from the Dehra Dun Academy, I was selected for admission to Sandhurst. On my return to India, I was commissioned into the Armed Forces of British India as a Lieutenant. I served until 1941.
	2. I was appointed Commander of the Household Guard of the state of D——. I held the ranks of Captain in the British Indian Army, and Brigadier of the Elephant Corps in the Army of D——.
	3. In 1943, I retired my commission, and was appointed Minister for Household Affairs to the Maharajah of D——.
	4. In 1945, I was appointed Treasury Minister to His Highness, the Nawab of N—— (another state in central India).
	5. In 1946, I was appointed Prime Minister to the Maharajah of D——.

6. In 1948, after the accession of D—— to India and the death of my father, I migrated to Pakistan and was granted a commission in the Pakistan Army. I retired as a Major in 1956.

7. I joined Messrs.—— (a Karachi manufacturer of textiles) as Sales Manager the same year. I left them in 1963, after having decided to settle in East Pakistan where a number of my relatives had gone.

8. I joined Messrs.—— (jute-millers in Dacca) as Assistant Sales Manager. My employers retrenched surplus personnel in 1967; and I was obliged to seek employment elsewhere.

9. I invested in a small wholesale business, dealing in jute, rice, and other produce. During the disturbances of 1971, I abandoned my business and returned to Karachi.

10. I am currently unemployed.

The personnel manager paused a long time over this application. He pictured impoverished royalty hawking his company's soaps and beauty aids to retailers in the bazaars of Karachi. He shook his head to clear it of images of a throneless prince who had bred elephants and served as ceremonial minister, who had come through the debacle of the princes in 1947 and had managed to survive on the periphery of the world of commerce until the political upheavals of 1971. He wrote to Major Nawabzada Mujibullah Khan:

Dear Sir,
We have considered your application for the post of Sales Representative in our organisation. We regret that we cannot invite you for interview at present. The position we wish to fill requires a younger man. Should any more suitable vacancy occur in the future, your application will be on our files.

Yours faithfully,

The "nabobs" (the British mispronunciation of *nawab*, or lord) was a term that covered a spectrum from royalty to petty grandees. With the decline of Moghul power, many taxation fiefs of the bureaucratic nobility became independent satrapies. Aristocrats set themselves up as ruling princes all over India, their states varying in size from sprawling Hyderabad, covering the entire Deccan plateau in South India, to tiny Baqua (a few villages on the borders of the UP and Nepal). In Punjab, the Sikh rulers created a new class of nobles by replacing the Muslim fiefholders with Sikh chieftains. The East India Company, which used the princes against one another in its expansion across the subcontinent, created a class of property-owning (as opposed to property-administering) landlords, first in Bengal and then in other areas under its control.

In 1857, in barracks near Calcutta, the soldiers refused the bullets of the new Enfield rifles, which were reported to have been greased with animal fat. The Muslim soldiers believed that lard had been used; since the pig is considered an unclean animal by Mussulmans, this was construed as a deliberate affront to their sensibilities. The Hindu soldiers believed that beef fat had been used; the cow being sacred to Hindus, this was a grotesque sacrilege to them. The Enfield rifles, with bullets greased with who knows what, were turned on the British officers. The Sepoy Mutiny had begun. The unusually harsh British reprisals, designed to prevent the revolt from spreading, had the opposite effect. Enraged mobs foamed into the streets of Calcutta.

The revolt spread across the subcontinent and escalated into a full-scale war of independence, for the nabobs seized the opportunity of rallying the people against the interlopers. This was the old order, the traditional concept of Indian society which the British had so rudely disturbed, reasserting itself. Telegraph wires, the symbol of the new domination, were pulled down, and engineers were hanged on telegraph poles. All over the subcontinent, hastily mobilized armies locked themselves in combat with the forces of the foreigner. Maulvis and Brahmins called on their parishioners to rise in revolt against the white man. The commanders of the liberation armies were Muslim aristocrats calling for restoration of the Moghul kingdoms to the emperor at Delhi, and Hindu rajas and noblemen with other, more ancient, aspirations. But there were many nabobs who did not join the revolt, and who used their soldiers to ensure the neutrality of their subjects. There were others who actively sided, or whose relatives sided, with the British, and who sent men and arms into action against their rebellious

In the streets of Quetta.

Hanging globes of mist
that hide the trees and fields
and coalesce to dewdrops
on the leaves.

133

countrymen. The land-deed barons in various parts of the subcontinent were creatures of the colonialists; their money and men were foremost in defending the trading area of the East India Company against the lordly rabble that sought to sunder it.

The fighting continued throughout 1857. The prime target of British rage was the last Moghul emperor, Bahadur Shah Zafar, who was by this time little more than a tourist attraction for visiting Europeans. Now this quiet, melancholy man became the inspiration for and the commander of rebel armies, the specter that haunted British nightmares. The battle for Delhi, the rebel capital, lasted from May to September. It culminated in a six-day siege, at the end of which the beleaguered population fled before the arson and murder unleashed by the victorious troops of Major-General Wilson.

Zafar was arrested by a Lieutenant Hodson, and for several months was confined under guard to the veranda of a courtyard in his palace. He sat there, exposed to the elements, until his trial and exile to Burma. As for the other members of his family, part of the story is told in the exultant narrative of Captain Charles Griffiths of Her Majesty's 61st Regiment of Foot:

Lieutenant Hodson . . . took prisoner, at a place some miles from Delhi, the two oldest sons and the grandson of the King. . . . Hodson's orders were precise as to the fate of these blood-thirsty ruffians, and though his name has been vilified and his reputation tarnished by so-called humanitarians . . . he was upheld by [men] better qualified to form a judgement than the sentimental beings at home. . . .
The three Princes were placed in a "gharee", or native carriage, and, guarded by Hodson's native troopers, were conducted towards the city. Before they entered, the carriage was stopped. . . . Dismounting from his horse and opening the door of the "gharee", [Hodson] fired two shots from a Colt's revolver into each of their hearts. After being driven to . . . the centre of Chandni Chauk [Chandni Chowk, the shopping street of Old Delhi] . . . the three bodies were stripped . . . and laid naked on the stone slabs.
Here I saw them that same afternoon; nor can it be said that I or the others who viewed the lifeless remains felt any pity in our hearts. . . . Two more sons of the old King were shot by sentence of court martial. . . . The 60th. Rifles . . . took, strange to say, such bad aim that the provost sergeant had to finish the work . . . with a pistol.

This particular execution was carried out before Zafar's eyes. His two youngest sons, whom he had believed safe, were decapitated. It is said that their heads were presented to their father on a silver tray, as part of a mocking *nazrana* (presentation of gifts to the emperor by one seeking an audience) by his captors. The revolt was fully suppressed everywhere within two months of the fall of Delhi. The war of independence, the last grand spasm of the old order, was over.

One after the other, selected nobles who had been prominent in the revolt were publicly hanged, crucified, or shot from cannon. Their families were deprived of their possessions and consigned to penury. Others were spared their titles and holdings, but were cowed into obedience by the ferocity of the exemplary punishment visited on their colleagues. Those lords and princes who had aided the British were awarded new satrapies, and the numbers of land-deed barons multiplied.

After the integration of the subcontinent under the direct control of the British Crown, two types of government were recognized: the provinces of British India, administered by London and Delhi, and the princely states. In the states, rulers were permitted to maintain a nominal independence, so long as they continued paying taxes. In fact, the actual task of governing these states was performed in most cases by British residents and appointees. The rajas and nawabs were encouraged to lead superbly opulent and indolent lives—they had the trappings, but not the substance, of power.

Without any real responsibility to their subjects, their incipient decadence became in some cases outright degeneracy. Then 1947 ended the ornamented splendor of the nabobs. The newly independent countries of India and Pakistan were not disposed—or able—to pamper royalty. Privy purses, specified in formal instruments of accession, and private estates maintained the fortunate ones in a semblance of their earlier luxury. Some were not as fortunate or shrewd; or they had fled their former states for one or the other new country and had to find lands or jobs or set up businesses or seek professional careers, just like everyone else.

In a crumbling mansion in Lahore, the very old widow of a former princely ruler in East Punjab remembers entertaining the late Duke of Windsor at tea

(left) Children of Quetta.

(above) At the tombs of the mirs, Hyderabad.

> And what is left? The ageless, crumbled splendor
> of one-time pride; the monuments of power
> inlaid with all the beauty wealth could buy
> to house a very human mass of bones.

137

when he was the Prince of Wales. When she was in her late sixties, this lady had a dream in which her dead husband appeared and commanded her to be always "as I remember you when we first married." She dresses now as a royal bride of the nineteenth century, in the flowing, silver- and gold-embroidered robes of a bygone era. In her wing of the house (the other wing is occupied by her eldest son, a well-to-do lawyer), she does not permit electric lights. She wanders around carrying a shielded candle; its light falls fitfully on the ancient family portraits before which she pauses. Her grandson used to tell his school friends that his house was haunted and take them at night—disbelieving and skeptical—to his grandmother's wing. As he walked the dark tapestry-hung halls, the schoolboy would suddenly encounter the other-worldly apparition of a silver-haired woman, dressed in the silks and brocades of an earlier age, carrying a candle. Yes, he would aver to other children the next day, the house is haunted.

The nawabs-reduced-to-commoners are not the only community of misfits in present-day Pakistan. There are other curiosa left over from the days of the Raj. There is a long-retired British colonel in Peshawar who spent his service life among Pathan tribes. His English colleagues wrote him off as having "gone native" back in the 1930s. Today he sits in the bar of the Peshawar Club and regales his fellow drinkers with tales from his days of greatness. He refuses to return to England.

In the streets of the mountain resort of Murree, an elderly Englishman and his wife are seen every summer, walking the twenty-two dogs who always travel with them. He was a general in the household guard of a nawab. He now lives on a pension from his days of service that may have been handsome when granted, but is quite inadequate for today's cost of living. So the couple make up by maintaining kennels of thoroughbred dogs. Their conversation revolves around the latest doings of the British royal family. They often talk of returning to settle in "good old England," but have always come back to Pakistan after their trips abroad.

One sees others from time to time, walking along quiet lanes in Lahore, Rawalpindi, and Peshawar—the baggy-trousered, handlebar-moustached remainders of the Raj, who belong neither in Pakistan nor in postcolonial England, with her miniskirts and uppity working classes.

Celebrating Eid, Old City, Lahore. At the Eid festival, the whole community gathers for prayer and a sermon in a large field at the edge of town or in an area known as Eidgah. Those who can put on new clothes, exchange presents and visits with friends and relatives, and give alms to the poor.

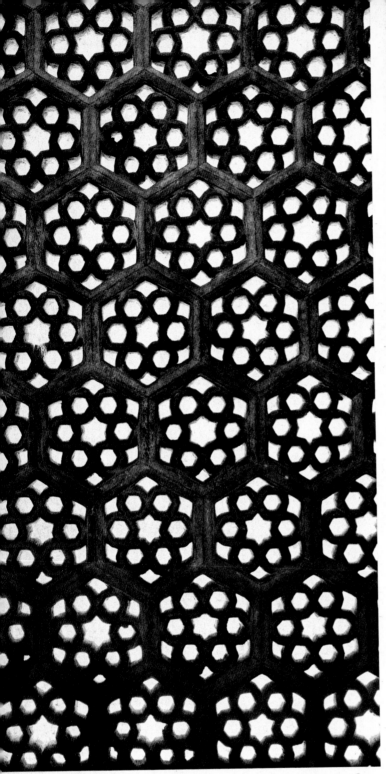

1, 2, 5. *Carved marble screens, Lahore Fort.*

3. *Naulakha Pavilion, built in 1633 by Shah Jehan. It is renowned for its extremely detailed* pietra dura *work.*

4. *Lahore Fort.*

(this page): The range of materials and skills that go into the decoration of trucks and carriages employs crafts rarely united in one trade. Wood, iron, steel, brass, cloth, silk, plastic, leather, oil paint, glass, ivory, and india rubber are used to transform the trucks that haul cargo over Pakistan's roads into dazzling flights of fancy on wheels.

(opposite page): The varied trades and textures of the marketplace, where people and goods mingle in a noisy, cheerful confusion of shapes, sounds, and colors.

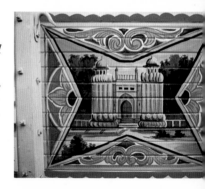

(left) Moghul arches, detail of Shish Mahal.
(above) Cleaning the marble reflecting pool, Badshahi Mosque.

4   Four Villages: Images and Realities

The Indus winds its slow way to the ocean from many springs in the mountains that house the northern valleys. It is dammed at many points and channeled and controlled by an intricate complex of barrages and canal headworks. It is thirty miles across at its widest point—a lazy brown sea broken by occasional sandbanks and islands. Where it finally enters the ocean, its mouths are trickles, undramatic leaks in the vast dike that is the irrigation system of the Indus Basin.

The water is needed by people, by crops, by trees, by flowers, by animals, by factories. It cannot be allowed to pour, uselessly and picturesquely, into the Arabian Sea. One of the world's great rivers must be sucked out of its bed and into the irrigation canals that keep 60 million people alive. The river takes its revenge. Not by destructive floods; the menace is more insidious. It is seen in fields so waterlogged that nothing will grow there except rank weeds and

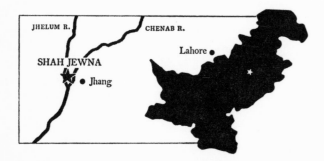

water plants. It is seen in fields turned pale and sterile with flaky saltpeter. Water has seeped through the walls of canals and risen in the subsoil, rotting the roots of standing plants. Water has brought up poisonous salts from below. This is the water that kills. At the opposite pole is the sheer insufficiency of water. Nearly half the land area is desert—sandy, rocky, or hilly. It is along the rivers, canals, and wells that people have put down their roots and made their homes. The waters of the Indus are the source of life, the constant pulse of this country, whether in the cities or in the ancient rural heartland of the people.

The greatest of the tributaries of the Indus is the Chenab. It rises in Tibet and flows into Pakistan from disputed Kashmir. Its waters flow past the old city of Gujarat, where they took the corpses of the lovers Sohni and Mahiwal. The Chenab is joined by the Jhelum near Jhang, and farther downstream it becomes one with the Ravi. Near the southern tip of the Punjab plain, the Chenab is joined by the combined streams of the Beas and the Sutlej, before entering the Indus in a magnificent confluence at the place known as Panjnad—"the five streams."

SHAH JEWNA

If the Indus is the river of history in this part of the world, the Chenab is the river of legend. The town of Jhang sits by its waters near where it is joined by the Jhelum; two miles from Jhang is the tomb of a woman called Heer.

In a village several miles away there lived a prosperous young farmer named Saida Khan Khera. The time was the middle of the fifteenth century. There was turmoil and disorder in the subcontinent, but it was far removed from this western corner of the Punjab plain. The passions that were to shatter Saida Khan's household were personal, not political; the forces that drove them were older than the thrones of kings and the ambitions of brilliant rebels.

A beggar knocked on the door of Saida's house one afternoon. His younger sister Sehti answered the door and saw a strange young man before her. He was nearly naked, except for a small black loincloth. His long hair was wound into a knot over his head, and he wore beads and heavy copper earrings. His face was pale and his form smeared with ashes and grime. But his body, despite the soot, was straight and strong and very beautiful; his eyes were disconcerting.

"No alms here," said Sehti, and pushed the man away. But this strange beggar resisted her push and, in the momentary confusion, his begging bowl fell with a loud crash to the stone step. Saida Khan's beautiful young wife, Heer, came running at the noise. She saw the beggar, stared at him a moment, and inexplicably fainted. The beggar quickly ran away.

The story had begun years before, when a daughter named Heer was born in the house of Chochak Sial, *mehr* (chieftain) of the Sial Rajput tribe of Jhang. She grew into an exceptionally beautiful girl, the pale skin of her perfect face pierced by her great, dark eyes. Many young men came to Chochak's house to ask for her hand, but he would play the gracious host and send them on their way. "My home will be less beautiful without my daughter," he would say.

Heer and her girlfriends passed the afternoons of her long youth by the banks of the Chenab. Sometimes they would bathe in its waters and sometimes float on a beautifully carved wooden boat. One summer afternoon, when the dust hung still on the air, Heer came down to the river with her friends. The only sound was the occasional, distant double note of a *koel* bird. It was very hot, and the soft mud of the riverbank cracked and flaked under their bare feet. A dark girl whom Heer did not know well was the first to get into the boat and discover the stranger. She had clambered over the side and was lowering herself onto the large bed when she saw a man sleeping there. Unnerved, she slipped and fell on him in a confusion of brown limbs.

The young man disentangled himself and began to apologize for trespassing. He had been very tired, he said. Heer's eyes wandered appreciatively over his face and form. He had extraordinary eyes and arresting hands. Her initial anger softened. "What is your name and where do you come from?" she asked. "I am Didhu," he said, "of the Ranjha clan. Since there are not many of my clan in these parts, my friends call me simply Ranjha. I come from Takht Hazara, which is three days walk from here." "Why have you come all this way to Jhang?" Heer asked him. Ranjha replied: "My father died and my brothers cheated me of my share of our lands. After that, they expected me to be useful on the farm; but I preferred to play the flute. So I left."

"You can play the flute?" exclaimed Heer. "Would you play something for us?" "With great pleasure," said Ranjha. As he delved in his bundle for his reed, the quiet girl who had first seen him cast the boat adrift. Ranjha sat up cross-legged on the bed. The girls arranged themselves around him. The notes of his flute rose, spare and poignant, into the sun-silenced air of the afternoon.

It was a hymn he played—a subtle, delicate hymn in praise of beauty and youth. The phrases were even, the melody exquisitely crafted. The girls listened entranced as Ranjha's superbly placed notes produced surprises in the melodic logic, leading them up first one musical pathway and then another. But the subtle hymn changed. A note of long, painful yearning intruded into its graceful structure. It was repeated, amplified, developed. Yearning took over the song—the ancient, insatiable yearning of youthful souls and beings. It became the song. The notes swelled to an ecstasy of unfulfillment, a painful, lyric fullness colored with glittering hints of an unendurable passion.

Suddenly, it stopped. Ranjha lowered the flute from puckered lips. The air was very still, palpable. The only sound was the river water lapping the sides of the boat. "If you're looking for work here," said Heer, breaking the silence, "come to my house. My father needs someone to tend his buffaloes."

So Ranjha became herdsman to the Sial mehr's cattle. All day he sat in the pastures as the buffaloes wallowed in the mud of the riverbank or grazed in the grass, and he thought the deep thoughts of youth. Each afternoon Heer would slip away from her friends and bring him food from her home. They would sit and talk and eat together. After eating, Ranjha would produce his flute and play for her. Ranjha told Heer the real reason he left Takht Hazara. "I had heard tales of the beauty of Chochak's daughter," he said. "I came to find you."

Inevitably people gossiped, and soon the whole town knew that Chochak's daughter was having a love affair with his herdsman. The whole town, that is, except Chochak himself. Heer had an uncle named Kaidu. He was lame in one leg and an embittered and vicious man. One day Kaidu limped to the top of a hillock. Hiding himself behind a bush, he watched his niece with the herdsman. When Heer came home, Chochak confronted her with Kaidu's story. She admitted the facts, but denied the details. Chochak, unconvinced, locked Heer in her room; Ranjha was forbidden to come near the house. "We should have married her off a long time ago," he fumed to his wife. They sent word to the chieftain of the Khera tribe in the nearby village of Rangpur that the suit he had sought for his son Saida Khan was now acceptable.

The Kheras came in a huge, joyful procession to fetch the bride. Rockets and pinwheels filled the skies. The town was a riot of color as people poured in from the surrounding villages in their wedding finery. The festivities went on for days, the noise and color filling all the senses, as Heer grieved silently in her chamber. Her cousins and friends came to bathe her on her *mehndi* night (the henna ceremony before the wedding day). They anointed her body with fragrant powders and oils. They combed and dressed her long hair and elongated her eyes with antimony. They dyed her hands and feet with red henna in intricate floral designs. Heer accepted all this in silence.

On the day of the marriage, Mehr Chochak gave a huge banquet. Before the Sial house, music played and people milled about. The Khera procession arrived. Saida Khan, almost invisible under the gold coins and woven roses of his *sehra* (headdress) rode a dark horse. Behind him his brothers carried the *doli*—the palanquin, embroidered with roses and myrtle and *champa* blossoms, in which his bride would return with him. Mehr Chochak greeted Saida Khan and embraced his father. The bridegroom was taken inside and shown his bride's face in a mirror. Outside again, he sat cross-legged beside his father-in-law-to-be as the *kazi* asked him in the presence of three witnesses, "Is this match accepted by you, Saida, son of Panna Khan Khera?" "It is," said Saida.

Then the kazi went inside to Heer. "Is this match accepted by you, Heer, daughter of Chochak Sial?" Heer looked at the quiet, bearded kazi. He was said to be a just and honest man, and it seemed a shame to startle him. But it had to be done. Very quietly, very firmly, she said, "No." "I beg your pardon," said the kazi. "No," said Heer, "the match is not accepted by me. I am betrothed to Didhu Ranjha."

Against her will, Heer was bundled into the doli and taken away by the Kheras. "The kazi is lying," she shouted, "I am not married." But nobody listened. As Saida's brothers began to carry her away, a long cry came from inside the screened compartment: "Oh, they are taking me away, they are taking me away after all!" But it was drowned in the noise of the music and singing.

At Saida Khan's house in Rangpur, the festivities continued late into the night, while Heer sat indoors on the flower-festooned nuptial bed. Finally, Saida Khan entered his bride's chamber. He sat down beside her and took her face in his hands. Heer said coldly: "Go away. You are not my husband. I have been brought here against my will." Saida had not been a witness to the scene before the kazi; he did not know that Heer was indeed not his wife. He thought she was only being difficult and withdrew. Heer lived on in Saida's house, his wife in all but reality. Sullenly, she went about her daily work, until the day her sister-in-law opened the door to a naked beggar. Heer recognized Ranjha, and fainted.

That night, when everyone was asleep, Sehti came to the distraught Heer's bedroom. Heer told her about Ranjha, and Sehti, in her turn, told of her own love for a Baluchi named Murad Khan. The girls consoled each other well into the night. Then they began to plan. The next day, as Sehti and Heer returned from the fields, Heer screamed, "A snake, a snake! I've been bitten by a snake!" People gathered quickly and helped the girls into their house. Sehti said (for this was all part of their scheme), "I know a young fakir who can cure snake-bite." "Find him immediately," said Saida.

Eventually Ranjha was shown into the room where the villagers were gathered around Heer's seemingly unconscious form. He sat down beside her and lifted her ankle to his lips. When he could not find the double mark of the deadly bite, he was puzzled. Then he understood. "I will need complete privacy to work my spells," he told the well-wishers. "Everyone must leave the room, except for you," he said, pointing at Sehti; "I will need your assistance." When the people had filed out of the room, Heer suddenly sat up and wept softly on Ranjha's shoulder. The three made their plans, and Ranjha left the house. "She is well now," he told Saida, and went in search of the Murad Khan of whom Sehti had told him.

On a certain night a week later, Sehti and Heer stole out of the house. Ranjha and Murad waited in the moonlight, and they were spirited away, leaving Saida Khan's house desolate and empty. Murad and Sehti rode away on a camel. Ranjha and Heer wandered on foot into a forest and lived there many days. But Saida and the Kheras caught up with them. The lovers fled across a tract of desert, then swam the Chenab and wandered on until they came to a city. The pursuing Kheras found them in the *caravanserai*. They beat Ranjha mercilessly with their staves and dragged Heer before the people.

"This woman is an adultress," they shouted. "Her husband has come to take her back." So Heer was taken to the court of the governor of the city. She fell at his feet and implored his protection. "This man is not my husband," she wept, "I was held at his house against my will." The governor's eyebrows rose. He had heard it all before. "Go on child, tell me your story," he said.

When he had heard her out, he thundered: "Adultery is a grave sin, and no one can condone it. No one can allow rightful homes to be polluted and sundered. The law is the law. You must go to your lawful husband." Heer quailed. Then he said in a softer tone: "But, my child, you do not have a husband from what you tell me. So you must return to your family until you are lawfully married. And I will come with you to ensure you do not withhold your consent this time. This is my condition, child. You must give your consent to the man your father has chosen for you."

So they returned to Jhang. The governor took Chochak aside and spoke to him for a while. Mehr Chochak emerged from his house and addressed Ranjha: "My son," he said, "go home." "I will not go without my bride," said Ranjha. "Go home, I said," continued Chochak, "go home and make preparations. Come with a proper marriage procession, and my daughter will be your bride." Ranjha left for Takht Hazara to prepare his wedding procession, and Mehr Chochak's house in Jhang was once again decked out for a wedding, a joyful one this time.

On the day of the marriage, Ranjha arrived with his doli. Perhaps his sehra and his procession were not as splendid as those of the Khera chieftain's son, but everyone was elated as they saw Didhu Ranjha radiant and smiling on his horse. Heer, in her chamber, heard the joyous lilt of the *shahnai* and the exuberant drums that told her the bridegroom had arrived. She smiled and sipped the glass of buttermilk which the quiet girl, the one who had been the first among her friends to see Ranjha, had brought her. It had a faintly bitter taste, but she did not notice it. Suddenly her breath began to catch in her breast, her vision to blur. Ranjha entered, surrounded by laughing girls, to look at his bride. Her lame uncle Kaidu snickered in the courtyard outside. Heer was dead.

She is buried near the town of Jhang. In the roof of her tomb is a large round hole just over her stone catafalque. In the monsoons, the raindrops patter through this hole, but her stone crypt is always dry. Only Ranjha's tears may wet her grave; and he wept them all before, as the legend goes, Heer's grave opened to allow him to enter and lie beside his bride forever.

Alexander the Great visited the place that was later to be the setting for the tragedy of Heer. His boats were wrecked in the strong current of the river, and many of his men were killed. The arrival of the Sial Rajputs, the dominant tribe in the area of Jhang, was less dramatic than that of Alexander. They came from the environs of Delhi sometime in the thirteenth century. Legend has it that they are descended from one Rai Shankar, who had three sons—Seu, Teu, and Gheu. Their descendants are, respectively, the Sial tribe, the Tiwanas, and the Ghebas. When Rai Shankar died, there was an intrafamily feud, and Seu left his home. He wandered over the plains to the distant town of Pakpattan. Here he met the famous saint Baba Farid Ganjskakr, who blessed Seu and worked miracles for his edification. Seu became a Muslim and returned to Jhang; his Sial descendants are all Muslims. There are many other smaller tribes and clans in the area. Most of these were brought to Islam in the sixteenth century and later by two different holy men, Shah Daulat and Shah Jewna.

During the long years of Moghul splendor, when the emperor Akbar was building his magnificent new capital at Fatehpur Sikri, a saintly fakir found his way to the Moghul court. This holy man's grandfather had come from Bokhara, in Central Asia, and settled in the region of the Panjnad. His grandson fascinated the Moghul court with his learning and his works before setting off again on his wanderings. He journeyed down the valley of the Chenab, and legend says he worked miracles as he went. His disciples called him Patay-Sewna (mender of the torn), since it was believed that he could make whole again anything that was rent, and heal the sick and wounded.

In the narrow triangle of land at the confluence of the Chenab and the Jhelum, he was greeted by the chieftain of the Marrals, a Ja'at tribe. The Marrals welcomed him as a saint and gave him a small area of land in which to live and teach. They called him Shah Jewna, the Living King. Shah Jewna was a syed, a descendant of the Prophet Mohammed. After the death of the Prophet, his father-in-law Hazrat Abu Bakr Siddiq had been elected as the first caliph of Islam. But the election had been held under emergency conditions. The Beni Hashim faction of the Quresh clan—the leading Arab clan, to which the Prophet belonged—felt that the Prophet's son-in-law, Hazrat Ali, was the more deserving candidate. Ali was a man of renowned piety and learning, and his authority in religious matters was acknowledged by Abu Bakr.

1–4. *The village of Shah Jewna and its surroundings.*

5. *Vigil. The* charpoy *(string bed) on which the woman sits is made of rope ingeniously wound around a wooden frame.*

6. *Returning from the mustard fields.*

7. *Weaver.*

8. *Straightening the warp.*

9. *Woodwork embellished with elaborate carving and with copper and ivory inlay is one of the traditional folk crafts of this area.*

8

9

The evening sunlight draws
from the waters and the earth
the vaporous essence
of fecundity.

1

2

3

4

5

6

1. Drummers summoning the procession.

2–6. Working on the tazia, *the elaborate papier-mâché replica of the martyr's shrine.*

7–10. Ashura, *the procession of the tenth of Muharram.*

1–3. *Ashura, the procession of the tenth of Muharram.*
4. *Pots of water are placed all over during Muharram to symbolize the cruel, thirsty death of the martyrs.*

Abu Bakr's election was upheld by the larger Beni Umayya faction of the Quresh. The impending controversy was laid to rest by Ali himself through his refusal to press his claim, and his acknowledgment of Abu Bakr. Ali's personal authority as a religious preceptor remained unchallenged during the reign of Abu Bakr and of the second caliph, Hazrat Umar Farooq. Umar was succeeded by Usman Ghani, and then the caliphate came around to Ali. But a schism had appeared in the time of Usman. Umayyad rulers had set themselves up, independently of Mecca, in Damascus. They paid only distant fealty to Usman's successor Ali, who derived his support mainly from southern Arabia and Persia. Ali made an agreement with Muaviya, the Umayyad ruler of Damascus, that after him Muaviya would acknowledge the spiritual authority of Ali's sons, the Imam Hassan and the Imam Hussain, the grandsons of the Prophet. When Hussain succeeded Hassan to the Imamate of Mecca, Muaviya, who had honored the agreement, was dead. Muaviya's son Yezid—known to all future generations of Muslims as a debauchee, a murderer, and an epic villain—was not disposed to acknowledge anyone's authority, spiritual or otherwise.

Hussain, promised support by the people of the Iraqi city of Kufa, which was part of Yezid's kingdom, set off for the city to rally the inhabitants to face Yezid. He took with him the twenty-seven men, women, and children of his family and household. When they reached the plain of Karbala, they received word that the Kufans had changed their allegiance. Hussain's party would have to stand alone against Yezid's host of thousands, for a mere hundred supporters joined him. On the desert plain beyond Karbala, the two forces met. For the first ten days, the first ten days of the Muslim New Year, the fighting continued until every last man, woman, and child of Hussain's tiny force had been massacred by Yezid's men.

All Muslims begin each new year by reliving the brutal martyrdom of the Prophet's grandson that split the Muslim world in two. The Shiah sect broke away, proclaiming that if Ali had been the first caliph, the seeds of this tragedy would never have been sown. The Sunni majority, while mourning the slaughter at Karbala, held the order of succession as legitimate and blamed Hussain's martyrdom on the villainy of Yezid. The descendants of Ali (and therefore of the Prophet's daughter) are known to Muslims by the title *syed* (or *sidi* or *cid*), which means "leader." Shah Jewna, whose ancestors had wandered from Mecca to Bokhara and thence to the subcontinent, was a syed. He converted the Marrals and all the resident clans of the area to Islam. He worked many miracles, so it is said, and a village grew where he lived. It is called by his name.

Near the grave of Heer, the Punjab winter day is balmy. The sunlight is sharp and warm, though the chill of the previous night still emanates from the ground. The earth is cool to the touch; but the deeper earth is warm and fecund to the million roots struggling downward in the fields lining the road. Green squares of cornfields, yellow-green of wheat, emerald green of mustard frothing to bright yellow blossoms, electric-blue flash of the *lungi* (sarong) worn by a passing girl—the land disassembles into a sunlit kaleidoscope on either side of the road leading southwest from Jhang. A high old orchard looms up; its shade envelops the road on either side. Small oranges, still green, and large limes hang from the branches in a bewildering profusion of plenty. The multiplication of colors that chessboards the land seems so natural, so easy. It tells nothing of the patient labor of centuries that has coaxed each hue from the stubborn brown earth. In winter the sky is a heart-rendingly bright blue; in summer it turns sheet white, lit by the constant heat flash of the sun.

The lushness is interwoven with the tall forms of men and women in the fields. A man and a girl—dressed in identical long black shirts and bright lungis —stand beside the road. He holds tools in his hands; she is carrying his hubble-bubble pipe for him. The colors of the country begin to dull to pale brown. Sad, sandy intrusions appear here and there, the occasional date palm and camels. The road becomes a dusty dirt track lined with low, white-trunked trees; beyond them the land is flat, the fields sparse. There are white patches of saltpeter. A bridge crosses a canal, and the road turns right. From this angle, Shah Jewna is like a desert village. Brown walls front on low sand dunes and a cluster of high date palms. A gaunt young man with hooded eyes pulls at his cigarette through a clenched fist. But the desert impression is misleading—or perhaps merely one of the reminders with which Punjab is replete. Beyond the village, where the lands of its inhabitants are, lushness suddenly multiplies again to a clash of color on the senses.

Behind the village is a canal. The quiet, hard-packed dirt road that runs along the top of its dike leads to the stud farms owned by the Bokhari family of Shah

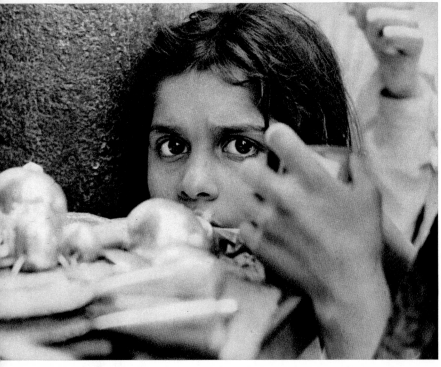

1, 3. At the majlis, *the traditional condolence meeting of Muharram.*

2. *Volunteer craftsmen spend the first nine days of Muharram building the tazia.*

169

Jewna. Their name denotes their origin, Bokhara in Central Asia. They are syeds, descendants of the saint who gave his name to this village, and the principal aristocrats of the area. The women of the Marral tribe traditionally work as midwives and governesses for the Bokhari family, and other clans plow their lands and pay them homage. Inside the gate of the village is a *maidan* (small square) fronted by houses on two sides and the marble *imambara* (Shiah mosque) on the side opposite the gate. Two doors down from the imambara is the tangle of the Bokhari houses—common walls and windows that look from one courtyard to the next, brick courtyard leading into brick courtyard—an aristocratic warren. The complex is crowned by the *havelis* (manors) of the makhdoom (custodian by descent of the shrine of the saint Shah Jewna) and the late Colonel Syed Abid Hussain Bokhari. The colonel was a cousin of the makhdoom and a leading citizen of the area. He was a famous figure of the subcontinent. A prominent young member of the Muslim League in the days before Partition, he played a notable political role in the freedom movement. After Partition and the creation of his new country, he continued in politics and served both as a legislator and as a cabinet minister.

Syed Raje Shah, Colonel Abid's father, had broken the family tradition by taking a non-syed wife, the daughter of a Bhatti Rajput chieftain. She suffered successive miscarriages which the household of his elder brother, the makhdoom, blamed on the departure from marital tradition. When his mother was twenty-four, the child who was to become Colonel Abid Hussain was conceived. Shortly afterward, Syed Raje Shah fell from a camel and died. The mother feared assassination. With the heir to Syed Raje Shah's estates in her body, she lived on a diet of milk, drunk directly from a buffalo. Four times a day, the widowed expectant mother would sit beside the buffalo while a trusted maidservant milked it in her sight. She would drink the milk and then return to her tense haveli. In the fullness of time, her son was born. She protected him fiercely until he grew to adulthood and could claim his property from the Court of Wards, which had administered the estate after his father's death.

Colonel Abid Hussain himself died without sons. His legacy devolved, in a total break with precedent, to his daughter Syeda Abida Hussain, who now performs the spirtual, temporal, and preceptory duties of the head of the Bokhari family of Shah Jewna. Abida Hussain's great passion is the stud farm her great-grandfather established. Here there are fields planted in clover, in which superb horses roam. It is unmanicured, uncoiffed. The clover and the grasses grow wild; the horses roam at will, and occasionally break into sudden, breath-taking gallops. It is like a dream of horses, where tall men in loose shirts and lungis groom and tend proud, exquisite animals.

The Bokhari havelis are the nucleus of the village, which spreads out in a loose, amoeboid shape with many straggling arms. The streets are clean, packed earth, unpredictably twisting between the sun-baked mud walls of houses. At the center is a noisy covered bazaar. During the first ten days of the lunar month of Muharram, these narrow streets are the stage for the many strange sights of the annual mourning ritual for the martyrdom of the Prophet's grandson.

MUHARRAM

Muharram is the first month of the Muslim year. Since the Muslim calendar is based on lunar months, it occurs at a different time each year. It was on the tenth day of Muharram that Imam Hussain's horse returned to camp without him. The first ten days of the month are therefore set aside by all Muslims as a period of mourning. For Sunnis (a little over half the population of Shah Jewna and the surrounding villages is Sunni), this is a quiet, home-centered affair. For the more ritual-loving Shiahs, the acts of mourning are an elaborate public ceremonial that climaxes in the singular frenzy of the morning of Ashura—the tenth of Muharram.

All the villagers wear black clothing throughout the month. Every day for the first ten days, *majlis* are held. A majlis is a condolence meeting at someone's house or at the imambara. Here, while the participants beat their breasts in unison, the virtues of Imam Hussain and the tales of his martyrdom are recited. At the end, dirges are sung. After the evening majlis, and after dinner, the Shiahs of the village gather in a prearranged street to enact a strange procession. The women form a hollow square, facing inward. In the starlit darkness of the country night, each woman is a black, indefinable shape; only the pale faces are discernible. They begin to chant long, indescribable dirges, the deliberate rhythm provided by their open palms falling against their breasts. The whole square of women shuffles in a sidewise motion, rotating gradually around its center, and

172

The village of Shah Jewna.

slowly moving forward in the narrow village lane. The earth-walled houses vibrate in time with the rhythm of the breast-beaters and of the drum thumped softly by the procession of men that follows behind the women. The men carry a *saje*—a flower-festooned mock coffin. This is a funeral procession. There is a separate funeral each night of the first nine nights of Muharram for the members of Imam Hussain's party killed on that particular day. Their way is lined by stalls dispensing water that symbolize the martyred Imam's wandering in the desert, where Yezid's men had poisoned all the wells. Eventually, the procession arrives at the imambara, and here the saje is laid to rest.

On the seventh night of Muharram, Imam Hussain had decided to marry his daughter to the son of his dead brother. Though he knew they were all to perish, he wished to honor his pledge and make the betrothed couple happy, if only briefly. Before the wedding ceremony could take place, an arrow from one of Yezid's snipers killed the bridegroom. So, on the night of the seventh of Muharram, after they have retired from the majlis and the saje of the evening, the Shiah women of Shah Jewna reemerge at 3 A.M. for a poignant mehndi procession. They congregate outside the houses of the Bokhari family. Here a large cake of henna has been prepared. It is decorated with flowers and colored paper and gold foil and is topped with lighted candles. The women carry the mehndi to the imambara, chanting melancholy songs lamenting the dead bride and groom. In the imambara, the mehndi is placed in the center and two or three hundred women sit around it, mourning. In the eerie light from the candles, only the ring of faces and the flash of hands rising and falling against chests can be seen. The only sounds are the crooning of soft *marsiyas* (dirges) and occasional uncontrollable weeping.

Early on the morning of the tenth, the women and their husbands begin a fast that is not broken until after the Ashura procession, and then with popcorn and tea. At ten o'clock on the morning of the tenth comes the climax of the Muharram ritual—the *tazia* processions. A tazia is a huge, elaborate papier-mâché monument, decked with gilt colored paper, that symbolizes the tomb of Imam Hussain at Karbala. It is carried behind a riderless horse. The tazias are built by volunteer craftsmen who labor for many days before. In Shah Jewna, three tazia processions are taken out—one by the Sunnis of the village, and one each by the two main Bokhari households, that of the makhdoom and that of Abida Hussain.

Each tazia starts at a different time from a different haveli. The three processions assemble one behind the other in the square opposite the imambara and carry the tazias outside the town for burial.

The procession of Sunnis moves to the sound of lamentations, but without *matam*—the ritual breast-beating and head-beating of the Shiahs. In the Shiah processions, matam attains a pitch of emotion unparalleled in the previous nine days. Clothes are rent, breasts and heads are beaten mercilessly until even the spectator reels with pain. Bare feet stamp the dust from the ground, and the constantly iterated cry "Hussain! Hussain! Hussain!" becomes a cosmic metronome. By this time the people of the village have worked themselves into an ecstatic frenzy. Some of the men have stripped to the waist and begun flailing themselves with thongs and chains and barbs and knives. They drive nails and spikes through their own hands and tongues. They draw blood from their eye sockets. They part their scalps with combs made from razorblades. The dusty streets become slippery, red mud paths.

The pond outside the village also turns bright red. This is where the mourners go to wash themselves and their self-inflicted wounds after the procession. It can only be these men's miraculous faith that guards their bodies from any sustained injury or infection. They emerge from the pond purged and expiated; the catharsis is over, the new year has begun. Donning clean black clothes, they rejoin the crowd in the maidan.

The Bokhari family, as descendants of the pir Shah Jewna, are the makhdooms of the village and surrounding areas. Technically this merely means that they are the custodians of the saint's grave and of his lands. In fact, this gives them a unique position in country society, a position that has much in common with that of the feudal gentry in Europe or Japan, but is fundamentally different. The Bokharis are landowners, yet their hereditary ownership of their estates is the product, and not the source, of their influence. They are not chieftains in any sense. Each clan has its own chieftain. Nor are they the official village functionaries. Each village has its own *chaudhri*, or headman, and the local governmental institutions are elected bodies. A Bokhari would have to stand for election like anybody else. They are not religious preceptors. The citizens of Shah Jewna have their own maulvis, as do the other surrounding villages. But the religious

1. Outdoor kitchens found in the courtyards of the houses of Shah Jewna.

2. The skill and care of the weavers of Punjab produce a rich variety of colors and designs using only simple looms.

3. Churning butter to fry parathas, *the delicious wheat bread of Punjab.*

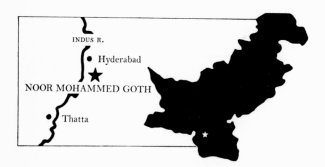

ceremonies of the saints and of Muharram will always begin from the Bokhari havelis, and no ritual would be complete without the participation of a member of the family. Their position means that they are the most sought-after, consulted, and relied-upon members of the community. The makhdoom family is not infrequently called upon to stop murders, solve feuds, advise farmers, and coax stubborn mothers-in-law.

The village and its surroundings are filled with legends and reminders of their saintly ancestor; even a mound of clay at the side of a certain street has a history and a lesson. Pir Shah Jewna had a grandson named Ladhan Imam. When Ladhan was fourteen years old, he is said to have been playing with some other boys about a furlong from the village. One of them taunted Ladhan to prove the claim that his family could work miracles. Ladhan walked across to a nearby wall, reached into a hole at its base, and pulled out a snake. He climbed astride the wall, cracked the snake as if it were a riding whip and, so the story goes, the wall rose like a horse from the ground, and the young miracle worker galloped away on it. He rode across fields and ditches till he came to the village.

In the streets of the village he was brought up short by the disapproving glare of his grandfather. The saint thundered his displeasure at his grandson's showing off: "These powers are given to us to advance the work of God," he said, "not to be dispersed at whim." He uttered a curse. The wall froze to a standstill; the riding crop became a snake again and slithered away. Ladhan Imam fell seriously ill and died two days later. The mound in the village street is the place where the wall stopped. It is called *pir ka ghora* ("the saint's horse"). The villagers come here to pray and to pay homage, and in May there is a festival to honor the memory of Ladhan Imam. In the worshipful respect paid to this unassuming mound of earth in a village street is much that is similar to the respect and awe in which the ordinary mortals of the makhdoom's family are held. They too exemplify history and heritage to the people of Shah Jewna; they are the link with a saint-hallowed, miraculous time.

NOOR MOHAMMED GOTH

In Punjab the old and the new blend naturally and intricately. Legends and the stories of saints are interwoven with ritual and the routines of daily life. The semifeudal institutions of the countryside are a product of the respect in which families of saints and holy men are held. Or they are the relatively recent creations of the largesse of the Raj. But for every feudal village, there are ten villages without a big landlord. And even within the estates of a nobleman, he is respected more for his person or his ancestry than for his economic position. Feudal institutions are not an organic part of village society; they are an outgrowth of it.

This is not as true in Sind. In these southern reaches of the Indus, life assumes a monumental character. A native flamboyance elevates custom to the level of ritual and transforms structures into brooding presences. Everything is a monument here, from the ruined squares of sinking Moenjodaro, to the subsiding melancholy of Thatta, to an ancient structure just outside Hyderabad at which children gaze with quiet eyes. In Sind a monolithic feudalism, organically wedded to clan ties and class distinctions, achieved its Asian flowering. The splendor of the medieval merchant barons was matched by that of the Sindhi country nobles. And their decline in modern times has been correspondingly spectacular. In pre-Partition days, wealthy Hindu merchants and bankers lived in the neighborhood of Hyderabad called Hirabad (Diamond Town). Hirabad today is a tenement area; its open drains run under the intricately carved balconies of former mansions. In Hirabad also are the tombs of the Talpur mirs, the last of whom lost Sind to the British Raj. The tombs cover a large area. They are blue and gold and green; the catafalques are white marble surrounded by marble filigree spelling the many names of God. The Talpur mirs represented the apex, the final flowering of feudal Sind. Their tombs are superb and melancholy, sublimely indifferent to the surrounding squalor.

The village of Noor Mohammed Goth is a settlement of the Kullachi tribe some ten miles from the little town of Tando Mohammed Khan in Lower Sind. It is a stone's throw from the village of Goth Behra, whose inhabitants belong to the Mirbehra clan. The Kullachis, once nomads in northern Baluchistan, have become settled farmers in Sind. However, this village seems to have maintained an itinerant character: it has had at least two previous locations, all on the estate of Wadero (landlord) Noor Mohammed Kullachi. There is no clear explanation for the periodic migration of masonry over the lands farmed by the inhabitants;

1. *Noor Mohammed Goth, end of a market day.*
2. *Ahmed Behra's guava orchard.*
3. *Grinding sugar-cane husks for fodder.*
4. *Cockfight, Noor Mohammed Goth.*

Clay balls—to swing from a long sling and frighten birds from the fruit. Noor Mohammed Goth.

Who speaks of Asian poverty? The tranquillity of orchards, the hubbub of bazaars, music and unique poetry—who is deprived?

185

1. *Women turn to primary colors—red, yellow, and black—to counteract the monotony of the desert. Sind.*

2. *Meher, the village belle. Sind.*

3. *The hand-blocked ajrak of Sind.*

186

perhaps it owes more to the nomadic folk origins of the people than to any easily identifiable economic or social causes. As the name of the landlord suggests, the village is not only physically mobile, but changes its name from generation to generation. During the life of the present wadero's father, it was known as Bashir Khan Goth. It will change its name again when Noor Mohammed's son succeeds him as wadero.

The Kullachis came to this region in the late eighteenth century. A Kullachi sardar, not an ancestor of this particular family of waderos, was awarded a *jagir* (estate) by a Talpur mir for meritorious service in battle. Much to everyone's astonishment, the hill chieftain was not pleased with this distinction. The Kullachis in ancient times were believed to have inhabited coastal lands near what is now the city of Karachi. The disappearance of forests and a reduction in numbers of livestock had driven them to the far northeastern corner of Baluchistan. This eighteenth-century sardar hoped to return to the coast. So he journeyed, with all Baluchi ceremony, to Hyderabad to renounce the jagir and claim what he considered his ancestral territory. The mir was astounded. His award spurned? Tribal claims on his seaport? He thundered his disapproval. Undeterred, the sardar threatened war. The mir deployed a regiment of troops—not to fight the Kullachis, but to ensure that their sardar took possession of the lands he had been granted. Fenced in on his estates, the sardar sullenly administered them. His children returned to the Kullachi homeland, and the estate lapsed to others.

Dissatisfied with his acquisition as the Kullachi sardar may have been, many of his tribesmen came and settled in and around the jagir. In due course, the jagir was parceled out in smaller estates, including that of the ancestors of the wadero Noor Mohammed. Noor Mohammed Kullachi's family live in Tando Mohammed Khan in a small, unimposing home on the outskirts of town. They have a country house not far from Noor Modammed Goth. It is a small place, used only on "business" visits to the land. On most days, the wadero motors out to his lands in his Russian-built jeep in the morning and drives back to Tando Mohammed Khan in the evening; or he comes for a hunt with his trained falcons.

The road leading to the village that bears his name is dusty and narrow. It winds between wheatfields and arrives at a small raised water channel. From the little footbridge crossing the water channel, one sees the rural elegance of substantial brick houses and a tractor standing beside a wall to the right. But,

1

2

*The subsiding splendor of ancient
Sind: 1. Thatta. 2. Hyderabad.*

says Ahmed Behra, this is Goth Behra. Noor Mohammed Goth is to the left. On the left are thatch houses and the brown smear of a high thorn hedge stretching in both directions. From a gap in the hedge a soft-spoken elderly man, barefoot and dressed in a gray army-surplus overcoat, steps forward. He is Sain Dino, the wadero or headman of Noor Mohammed Goth (in Sind both the landlord and the village headman are called "wadero"). The winter day is surprisingly warm; the sunlight is a flat, even white. How can he bear the overcoat? But Sain Dino is undaunted by the warmth. He is poor, but the collar and hem of his overcoat have been embroidered with a delicate tracery of colored threads. The village behind the hedge, beyond which strangers are not permitted without the headman's leave, at first appears poor. The houses are thatch and upright timbers, with few brick or mud walls. But the impression of poverty is misleading. Thatch and timbers are used not so much for economy as for climatic reasons, as well as ease in relocation.

Sain Dino's brother Sain Ditto is a huntsman. He owns a long, ancient musket with which he boasts he can bring down a rabbit at a hundred paces. He is an old man now, and almost blind. He cannot see to walk about unaccompanied, so his little grandson leads him. Yet he still goes out periodically and shoots wild pigs. "I aim at the noise," he says, "pigs make a great deal of noise." "But pigs are dangerous animals," he is asked, "what if one of them gores you with his tusks?" "They will not," he answers, "I will hear the noise first." In the shed of a house is a pig that has been caught but not killed. Through a window one is treated to a glimpse of a razor-backed beast with four-inch tusks. It snorts and snarls as its small, sharp hooves plow the ground.

But Muslims never keep pigs. They never touch even the corpses of the wild pigs shot in the fields. Ahmed Behra says, "Pigs are a great menace in the fields. They uproot crops and destroy standing wheat and sugarcane. A pig mauled a woman to death just the other day." But aren't his people Muslims? Why do they keep this pig instead of killing it? He shrugs: "I don't understand it either; there's no accounting for it. In any case," he smiles, "these are not my people. I live in this goth, and Kullachis work my orchard. But I am a Mirbehra. My people live in Goth Behra, the neighboring village."

The Kullachi village follows no logical layout. Houses of straw and thatch with deep verandas proliferate at random. The streets are merely the spaces that are not buildings or fields. In the evening, after the warmth of the day, a cool, moist breeze suddenly springs up. The breeze has a faint but distinct salt tang. There are sea gulls in the sky. How far from the sea are we? "A hundred and thirty miles," says Sain Dino.

Morning in Noor Mohammed Goth begins early. At dawn a muezzin calls for prayer from the village mosque. It is very cold and very dark, except for a thin strip of pearl along one edge of the horizon. There are sounds of shuffling people, waking children. As cooking fires are lit, the morning air turns blue and astringent. Through the smoke and the river mist of early morning, dark figures find their way to wash in the icy water of the nearby canal. By the time day breaks fully and white sunlight washes the dry landscape, the village is almost empty of its menfolk. When a family's field is ready for harvest, the women and children go into the fields with the men. They leave the houses open and unguarded. If a house is locked, it means the man has died and his family has moved away.

Thorny scrubs and sandy outcroppings fringe and interrupt the lush green wheatfields. A ripening patch of sugarcane marks the horizon. Shapes of women bringing their husbands the mid-morning meal undulate along the dike of the canal. It is a horizontal composition stressed by vertical forms. The Sindhi plains stretch, flat and incredibly ancient, all around. Even the winter sunlight is full of glare from the ever-present dust in the sky. And it is surprisingly warm.

Ahmed Behra's orchard is a blissful retreat. Its deep green shade, where groups of men pluck guavas and limes from the lower branches, is sensuously delicious. At each corner of the orchard is a tree-high platform on which a man stands slinging small clay balls from a long cord that cracks like a gunshot. The whip-lash sounds and the thump of the ammunition are accompanied by an occasional long, loud cry—all to frighten crows away from the fruit. In the village, in the evening, the buffaloes return from the canal. They loom in a mass into the little streets; black, mud-flaked hell-creatures with staring, china-blue eyes. They are flanked by a covey of defenseless-looking children harrying them to their respective homes.

A ponderous buffalo emerges,
clambering slowly from his mud pond; his gunmetal flanks

steam blue clouds into the yellow light.
His china-plate eyes are confused; his fearsome
muscles twitch, shivering
at the needle touch of winter air.

A little boy
cradles goose-pimpled feet in his hands, his vapourous breath
hangs before his face. The air
is sharp with evening smoke of wood and cow-dung.
The crisp, blue exhalation of a human village
settles unmoving around the silent tree trunks.
The buffalo's eyes glaze over.
pondering alternatives of comfort; he pauses
and settles back into the warm, dung-richened mud.

The houses of the village are huddled together
in the cold, golden light of sunset,
like sheep without a fold.

SALMAN TARIK KURESHI

The character and texture of Noor Mohammed Goth are completely Sindhi, except for occasional, lingering traces of the nomadic past of the inhabitants, a past now forsaken for nearly two centuries. Occasionally, though, the villagers are greeted by some of their long-abandoned Baluchi "cousins." A group of herders from the Marri clan in eastern Baluchistan had wandered out of their hills and settled between Noor Mohammed Goth and the neighboring village of Goth Behra. The two villages share a common *lambardar* (numbers man, keeper of land records), who lived in Goth Behra. Kallo Khan, the headman of the Marri wanderers, became a close personal friend of the lambardar.

The sheep and goats of the Marris cropped the stiff grass and thorny scrubs in the nearby common pasture and kept the hedges of Noor Mohammed Goth and Goth Behra trimmed. Peaceful coexistence between the herdsmen and the farmers was the rule: but the animals began to stray into the fields and eat the standing crops. No one could, of course, say for sure whether these were the animals of the nomads or of the villagers, but popular feeling seemed to go against the newcomers. Sain Dino, on behalf of his own villagers, complained to Kallo Khan. The latter said with a shrug, "You can't explain property boundaries to animals." Sain Dino and the other villagers protested to the lambardar. But he only said, "Kallo Khan is my friend. I will do nothing against him or his people." The situation worsened. There were quarrels, and occasional fights. The friendship between the lambardar and Kallo Khan became strained. The villagers threatened reprisals on the herdsmen. Finally, a conclave was called. Kallo Khan and the lambardar sat down to negotiate, as the spokesmen for the two sides, while the others gathered around to listen.

"Since you are my friend," began the lambardar, "I will not ask you and your people to move away from here. But I must insist that you keep your animals within the grazing grounds."

"The animals will go wherever they find something to eat," said Kallo Khan. "Since you are my friend, I must ask you to accept the fact that they will stray."

"Since you are my friend," said the lambardar, "and I do not want to spoil our friendship, I will have to ask you to kill off your animals."

Kallo Khan said: "Then we may as well kill ourselves off. The animals are our only livelihood. Since you are my friend, I must ask that your people kill their animals off; then there will be enough in the pastures for us."

The lambardar answered: "That is impossible. Since you are my friend and I wish to preserve our friendship, I must ask you to graze your animals somewhere else."

"That will involve a wasteful daily journey," said Kallo Khan. "We always graze our flock where we live. Since I wish to preserve your friendship, we will simply move away from here."

"My concern is the welfare of the village folk," said the lambardar. "Since I also wish to preserve our friendship, I am forced to admit that you must go away from here; otherwise our friendship will become impossible."

At this, the listening villagers interceded. The arguments of the two friends seemed to come to only one unfortunate conclusion. "Why not simply guarantee that the herds will only graze the pastures and not the foodbeds or fields? If these pastures are insufficient, we can make more land available. But they don't

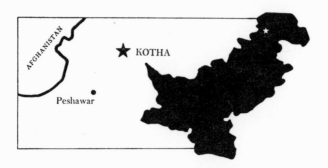

have to move away." The two friends were happy. Why hadn't they thought of this before? Peaceful coexistence was preserved.

KOTHA

It is a long journey from the desert-fringed plains of Sind to the mountains of the Northwest Frontier Province of Pakistan. If the journey begins in Karachi, the traveler takes a plane or catches the Khyber Mail Express. The train makes its thirty-six-hour way over nearly twelve hundred miles of track. It passes through desert and farmland, town and village, orchard and forest. There are long nocturnal halts, when one wakes to the blue light of country station platforms, the sound of shuffling feet, and the cries of people selling hot eggs and tea and cakes.

The train travels the length of the dusty, desert-fringed plains of Sind, and across the greener plains of Punjab. From Lahore it turns northwestward. It crosses the Ravi and passes the sprawl of industrial towns above Lahore. The farmland beyond is lush and controlled. It crosses the Chenab. Beyond Gujarat, low, dry hills begin to appear, then the river Jhelum; then the high, gully-cut plains of the Potwar plateau, higher hills in the distance, Rawalpindi.

The train turns almost due west, following the track of the Grand Trunk Road, which the fifteenth-century emperor Sher Shah Suri built from Peshawar to Lahore and to Multan, and from Lahore across the subcontinent to Calcutta. The track winds up into high hills and then leaps dramatically across the Indus at Attock. Ten miles above Attock, Kund Island in the middle of the river separates the commingling streams of the Indus and its Kabul River tributary. The Kabul, which has wound through the Peshawar valley, is blue with streaks of brown; the Indus, fresh from the mountains, is white. For many miles below Kund, the western half of the Indus is blue and the eastern half white, until they merge into a single watery shade below the high walls of the fort built by Sher Shah Suri on the foundations of the fort built by Babar on the ruins of the fort built by Mohammed Ghauri on the remains of the fort built by Asoka, above Attock.

The track follows the Peshawar valley to the ancient city of that name. From Peshawar, a car travels back along the Grand Trunk Road for twenty miles and turns left at Nowshera. Snow-capped mountains are the backdrop of this, the Mardan valley. The land bristles with sugarcane and subsides into waving tobacco fronds. Then the mountains rise and climb, reaching toward the gap called the Malakand Pass. The mountains are black, bare; but, as one passes Malakand and begins to descend into the Swat valley, the sides are clothed with the green of grass and trees and an embroidery of poppies and narcissus. In the valley, the river Swat meanders over beds of white pebbles, and there are fields of corn, mustard and saffron, and high poplars and pines. There are emeralds in the mountain mines that are believed to tumble sometimes, in glittering deep-green facets, down the cascades of the river.

Three centuries ago there lived a malik of the Yusufzai tribe called Hassan Khan. His son Adam Khan was handsome and strong. He rode and hunted well and was a skilled marksman with the musket. He was a champion wrestler, in spite of his slim form. But there was a gentler side to Adam Khan's nature. Also a musician, he played the *rabab* (a kind of lute) and sang long ballads about chivalrous men and proud, beautiful women. One sunlit morning, the villagers gathered for a wrestling match between Adam Khan and Meermai, the mountain chieftain. Meermai was older, but his strength and skill were famed; his tall, stocky frame was topped by a surprisingly gaunt face. He seldom came down from the mountains and was feared in the valley for the band of desperadoes he led. Because Hassan Khan had once done him a service, he had accepted Adam Khan's invitation.

In the stony village square, Meermai towered nearly a head above the tall Adam Khan. His great shaggy form seemed to envelop the youth as the two men, dressed only in *shalwars* (loose pantaloons), stood facing each other. The referee passed the double belt around their waists and bound them together. They grasped each other's arms and the match began. With a quick kick, Adam threw Meermai off balance, and he fell to the ground, dragging Adam Khan on top of him. But Adam could not seal the advantage; within a few seconds he was face down with Meermai on his back. Adam threw Meermai off and slithered upright. Their bodies pressed together, they strained at each other for a long while; but neither gave way. Then Adam grasped Meermai's leg and threw him over. His wrestling belt pulled the bandit chief up with him again. Standing now, the sweating forms were locked in a muscular embrace. Gradually Meermai pushed Adam farther and farther back until the boy's head was almost touching the ground behind him. With a sudden movement, Adam freed himself, darted forward between Meermai's legs, and quickly raised the bandit off the ground on his shoulders. Meermai thrashed wildly, but it was over. His feet had left the ground.

An elated Adam rode off into the hills. But then his horse threw a shoe, and he was forced to stop at a village to have it reshod. While the blacksmith worked, Adam rested on a rope cot under a tree in front of the smithy's shop. He leaned back; he smiled up at the sky. Taking up his rabab, he struck a few notes and began to sing. It was an ancient Pathan song that he sang, a song about a boy who wandered free in the mountains and about the dark-eyed girl who brought him back to the quiet splendor of the valleys. A crowd gathered to listen.

In this village lived a man named Taoos Khan. His name meant "peacock," and he was known for his proud, extravagant ways. Taoos had a daughter named Durkhane, who happened to go that day to the smithy to have the spindle of her spinning wheel sharpened. She heard the singing, saw the crowd, and stopped a little apart from the others to listen. Presently the blacksmith brought the reshod horse back. Adam finished his song, mounted, and began to ride away when he suddenly saw Durkhane. She was dressed in black, and the alabaster white of her face was framed by her dark hood. Adam's gaze fell to her soft white hands and rose again to her quiet, gray-green eyes. Durkhane modestly dropped her gaze and hurried into the blacksmith's shop. That evening, Adam sat up late in his room, strumming his rabab, unable to sleep. Finally, he fell into a deep, exhausted slumber.

Adam normally went to his father's room each morning to wake Hassan Khan and to press his legs. But that morning he overslept. When his eyes opened, the sun was high and his father was standing beside his bed. The boy rose, apologizing for having missed his filial duty. "My son," asked his father, "are you ill? You have never slept so late before." Adam insisted he was well. But, in the following few days, he was distant and absent-minded. Hassan Khan was convinced that his son was either ill or possessed. He pressed Adam to visit the *hakim* (doctor). Finally Adam said: "Father, I am not ill; I am overjoyed. I have seen the girl I want to marry." He described Durkhane, and the brief meeting of their eyes. Hassan went to his own room and thought for a while. Then he sent for his son's closest friends, Meero and Ballo. He said: "Go and find out who this girl is. Seek out her father and tell him that Hassan Khan, chieftain of the Yusufzai, pays his compliments and desires the hand of his daughter for his only son Adam Khan."

Meero and Ballo journeyed to the village. The smith there remembered the girl in black who had visited his shop on the day in question. "She is Durkhane, the daughter of Taoos Khan, the richest man in our village," he announced. So they went to Taoos Khan, who received them graciously and bade them eat with him. But he regretted that he could not entertain the suit, since his daughter was already betrothed to a man called Payao.

One day many weeks later, while the preparations for her wedding to Payao were being made, Durkhane sat at her spinning wheel. As she pondered over the manly young musician she had seen so briefly, she was visited by an aging aunt of hers. After inconsequential talk of this and that, her aunt told Durkhane that she had come with a message from a young man who loved her passionately.

"Who is he?" asked Durkhane.

"His name is Adam Khan, son of Hassan Khan. He saw you one day when he came to our village to have his horse shod and sat outside the smithy singing a song."

"And what is his message?" she asked.

"That he wishes to meet you, alone."

"Tell him that I share his feelings but that I am already betrothed. Nevertheless, I will meet him."

A few nights later, when Taoos Khan was away on business, Adam arrived at Durkhane's house. For some time, they did not speak a word; they only gazed at each other in bewilderment and joy and anguish. Then Adam took Durkhane's hand in his. Slowly the night passed. One by one, the stars began to fade, the early morning breeze to blow. It was dawn. Adam rode back to his village.

It was a few days later that Durkhane was married to Payao, and went to live in his opulent home. Adam rode into the hills to meet Meermai. He and the bandit chief engaged in a long conversation. The next day, Meermai and his men rode down on Durkhane's village. The people scattered and ran. But the bandits stopped only at Payao's house. They took his young wife and rode away.

1

2

1. *An informal bus depot, a place for passengers and drivers to stretch and refresh themselves. Tribal area, NWFP.*

2. *Kotha.*

3. *Schoolchildren, Kotha.*

3

197

1. *Schoolgirl, Kotha. The ancient art of calligraphy will be taught her on these slates.*

2. *The village storekeeper, Kotha.*

3. *A member of the tribal jirga, Kotha.*

4, 5. *Around Kotha.*

6. *School break, Kotha.*

5

6

2

3

1. *Young hunters, Kotha.*

2. *The pattern of embroidery on a Pathan woman's* chadoor *(shawl) identifies her tribe.*

3. *The secret of modesty is in the eyes.*

1. The camel is pack animal, transport, and source of milk; it is an intrinsic part of human life in the vastness of Baluchistan.

2. Putting out to sea, Gadani.

3. Looking for seashells to clean and polish and sell when the annual mela (festival) occurs, Gadani.

4. Fishermen, Gadani.

4

(*above*) *Running to meet the fishing boats, Gadani.*
(*right*) *Net maker, Gadani.*

1

2

1. *Sunset, Gadani.*
2. *Children, Gadani.*
3. *On the beach at Gadani.*

Baluchi girl.

They informed her husband that she would be kept at their stronghold, among Meermai's womenfolk, until Payao agreed to divorce her. Adam, when he heard the news, went again to the bandit's lair, this time to meet his beloved.

But Payao and Taoos Khan had come there before him, with gold and sheep and horses and guns for Meermai. When Adam arrived, he found that the bandit had accepted the ransom and handed Durkhane back to her husband. To a heartbroken and bitter Adam Khan, Meermai said: "Do not force me to violate the ritual of hospitality. I give you three hours to be out of my territory." Adam wandered in the mountains and came to a cliff. Silently, he stepped off the edge and fell to the rocks below. Durkhane, when she heard the news, went into a decline. She recovered briefly when, at her request, Adam's friend Meero came and played Adam's rabab for her. But slowly she faded and weakened and died. Her people buried her with her lover.

Pathan social formations are different from those of the plains. Among Punjabis and Sindhis, village life for centuries was governed by *panchayats*, elected councils that had both judicial and legislative authority at the village level; executive and police authority resided with local headmen—the chaudhri in Punjab or the wadero in Sind—appointed by the councils. The societies of the plains certainly had clan and tribe origins, but these authority patterns had broken down centuries before, and the village had long been the unit of society. Not so among the Pathans, where the tribe is still the unit of society, even outside the "tribal areas" proper. Traditionally, the various villages of a particular tribe would elect a jirga, or council of elders, to make moral and legal decisions and elect the tribal chieftain (the khan or the malik). Each village of the tribe maintained a patch of communally farmed land, the *khankhel*, the produce of which went to maintain the khan and free him from material concerns. At the village level, the direct participation of every man in the dera served the purposes of local community organization. The entire conceptual emphasis of such an organization was different from that of the plains people.

The three main dialect groups of the Pathans are divided into various tribes and septs. Afridi in the Khyber Pass, Mohmand in the Malakand area, Wazir in Waziristan, Mahsud in Kohat, Tareen in Hazara, to name some. By far the largest Pathan tribe are the Yusufzai of the Mardan and Swat valleys. The

Yusufzai claim to have come from the environs of Kandahar in Afghanistan. They trace their ancestry from one Othman of Kandahar who had three sons: Ali, Kana, and Aka, whose descendants are, respectively, the Alizai, Kanazai, and Akazai septs of the clan of Othman. The Alizai are in turn divided among the Samakhel, Ismailkhel, Bubakhel, and Punjpaoi subsepts, named after Sama, Ismail, Buba, and Punjpao, the four sons of Ali.

The Yusufzai settled in the Mardan and Swat valleys and the surrounding hills. The Mandaur Yusufzai subclan established themselves in four principal villages: Topai, Mehnai, Batakurra, and Kotha. Kotha is in the hills that fringe the north of the Mardan valley. It is a sizable village of some three thousand people. From the outside, it presents a fortress appearance, for the walls of the stone houses on the periphery have no doors or windows.

There are two rainy seasons here, a long monsoon at the end of summer and a short rainy spell at the end of winter. The winter winds come down from Central Asia, picking up their moisture from the Caspian Sea; they turn along the path of many different invaders, through the passes of the Hindu Kush. The Khyber at this time of year is clogged with cloud. The clouds spread out again below the pass, opening out into the great subcontinental funnel. The northern mountains are a passless wall; the clouds dissolve in rain on their sides and run into the valleys. Streams and rivers swell, fed by the rains and the early-melting snows, and flow into the welcoming tides of the Indus. The river Swat is a rushing torrent. The water is clear as air, patterned with the white froth of its rapid passage. The pebbles of the riverbed are white; they move slowly, hectically, driven by the force of the water, until they pile up on top of one another in glittering dams over which the waters break in small cascades. At the foot of the Swat valley, the grim mountains of the Malakand range are lost in the smoke of rainclouds.

One loses sight of the world. The steep, winding road is invisible, but for a tiny horizon the width of two windshield-wiper blades. The tall figure of a man, his high nose and red-dyed beard almost meeting like the arms of a nutcracker, trudges past. He is bent double with the driving rain and the steepness of the slope. His gray eyes are mocking. "What are these city fools doing driving on treacherous mountain roads in weather like this?" What is *he* doing, walking in the rain in the middle of nowhere?

On the southern slopes of the Malakand range, the road descends through layer after layer of cloud and mist to the Mardan valley. From the small town of Jahangira, a branch road goes off to the right; it climbs up into the hills again before reaching Kotha, not far from the emperor Ashoka's provincial capital near Shergarh. In the cloudy distance behind Kotha is the silhouette of Mount Khuraman. On its level back, in the old days, a fire was lit whenever it was necessary to call the Yusufzai tribe together.

When the four towns of the Mandaur Yusufzai were established, the land surrounding each village was farmed communally. Each plot (or *wand*) was divided into portions called *shershai*. A shershai was a strip of land running the length of the plot, and its width was the distance between a man's toes when he stands with his heels joined at right angles to each other. Each member of the village was given a shershai in each of several wands to ensure that no one man would have more or better-quality land than another. Sowing and cultivation were entirely communal operations, the whole village farming the lands as a group. The shershai was important only for the harvest. At the time of harvest, each man took the produce only from his allotted shershais.

To the Pathan of those days attachment to property and accumulation of wealth were rather undignified practices. The Pathan code was honor, of the tribe and of the individual. Material wealth was not conditioned by honor. Even a dishonorable man could accumulate wealth. So the inhabitants of Kotha and its brother villages did not grow cash crops and crops to sell—only food grains and vegetables enough for themselves, and a little extra for the stipends of artisans and craftsmen and for the stores of the khankhel. To further render money unnecessary, each family had its own milk animals and produced strong and healthy children. As a final discouragement to attachment to material possessions, the entire population of each of these four villages was frequently rotated.

But times, and property relationships, changed in the nineteenth century. The British had become the new arbiters of the subcontinent and had taken control of the Mardan valley. They brought with them, in their mission of "civilizing the world," the concepts of hereditary ownership of property and hereditary authority. In the lands of the Yusufzai, the British threw up their hands in horror at their untidy, undocumentable ways of administering society and property. It was impossible that there should be productive lands not owned by anyone. The Raj needed to collect taxes. Where were the documents or traditions that showed who owned what, so that rational assessments and collection could be made? The khan of the tribe died, and British observers were shocked to see that there was no ready succession. The jirga sat and deliberated for many khanless weeks before they appointed a successor. The new khan was controversial; opinions were divided as to his worth. But the minority faction did not mind. "If he proves incompetent," they said, "the jirga will see our point and elect a new khan."

No lifetime tenure, no hereditary principle of authority, no easily definable property relationships—this was unworkable. It contradicted the most fundamental social premises of Victorian England. It must change. By decrees, the khankhels were converted into the personal property of the current khan, inheritable by his children. This upset the age-old balance between the khan and the jirga, which further lost when the new government threw its weight behind the son of the khan as the inheritor of the title, regardless of what the jirga might rule. Overnight, traditional authority and property relations among the Yusufzai fell apart. The modernization of the Mardan valley had begun. The khans became landlords; fathers willed property to sons; people accumulated the unneeded, heretofore unpossessed, segments of land. Some became wealthy, others remained poor. The basis of society had changed.

Kotha today is a prosperous village. The inhabitants grow tobacco for cigarette factories and sugarcane for the sugar mills in nearby Takht-i-Bhai and Mardan towns. Merchants and businessmen negotiate with individual landowners and tenants for the sale of their produce. The government collects taxes, and all is just as it should be. Farmers own transistor radios, but they can still trace their lineage back to Othman.

Air Conditioned Compartment

The neutral voice,
with only the gentlest pressure, the finest inflexion,
on a falling final vowel,
     my fellow traveller
(elegant, precise),
   your intellect flows

in words, selected, in a polished commentary
on all you consider significant today.

And what do I gather, Mr. What-was-your-name?
what do I glean?
                    I mark the rising gesture,
your hand's transcendant arc. "The Government
can give the nation only what it accepts."

You cross your legs;
you lean back. "And who needs Referenda?
Freedom . . . Responsibility . . . must radiate from the pinnacle
and filter through the inner being of the masses."

A camel beside the tracks and his rider
gazing (an age-old lassitude, a brutal boredom)
at the row of windows rattling past them.

"This is the only genuine experience." Your hands held
parallel before you.
parting firmly, persuasively. "This . . .
the Consciousness spreading downwards
with corrosive violence. This is the INTELLIGENT Revolution,
whose seismic shock-waves—and this is the sign!—rebound
against a natural Reaction to Stability."

Your significant nod punctuates the phrase.
  (Thorn and Acacia,
  the date-palm,
  in the dry sands,
               reaching . . .
                             downwards . . .)
Your literate eloquence adds the capital letters.

"A useful commodity, Progress—you know it's there
when it sets up this Questioning,
this Reaction, against itself and Stability.

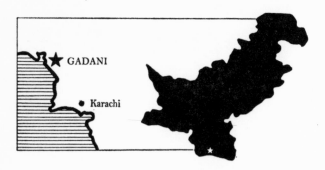

The thoughtful man compares today's position
with what it was some years back, and we're still very young."

Flat skyline
and flatter fields, saltpetre and the faded sands.

"Yes, young and vigorous; We're in the process of manufacturing
a glorious History."

Your emphatic hand
severs the lingering thread, and six thousand years
are cancelled.
        (And that sun outside . . .
that bleaching, corroding, blasting monster-sun . . .)

SALMAN TARIK KURESHI

GADANI

The mountains of the NWFP run, with the main trunk of the Hindu Kush, into the hills of Baluchistan. Pathan villages and towns are continuous in these mountains, all the way to the provincial capital of Quetta. But it is not that easy to travel from Kotha to Quetta. There are few passable roads or railway lines through the mountains. In a land of such dramatic geography, modern communications must compromise with nature. To get from the mountains to the mountains, one must cross the plains. One can drive to Peshawar, fly from there to Rawalpindi, change planes and fly over the plains and hills, stopping at Lahore, Lyallpur, and Multan, before reaching the high airstrip at Quetta. Or one takes the Quetta Express from Rawalpindi. It is a thirty-hour journey from Punjab to Baluchistan. The train beats its way across the five-river plains and into Sind, turns west from Rohri, through Sukkur, and draws itself toward the dry little town of Jacobabad. Beyond Jacobabad, it crosses the Baluchistan border near Jhatpat.

This is the plain that skirts the northeast of the Baluchistan hills. The land is green (although there are frequent dusty intrusions), watered by the recently dug Pat feeder canal. This too was desert, until the canal and its attendant water channels were brought here all the way from the Indus River. Small farms and villages now dot the landscape where there were only rock-strewn sand dunes before. Here, civil disorder has come with the new-found fertility. Ancient and conflicting tribal claims on the Pat lands had remained quiescent in its desert days. The clans skirted each other, with only occasional skirmishes. But water brought a potential for wealth, non-Baluchi people in search of farmland, and an intensification of tribal land hostilities.

At the extreme point of the Pat plain is the town of Sibi, the hottest city in Pakistan. In summer, temperatures soar to over 125°; in winter, the biting winds off the barren mountains bring a bone-freezing chill. The plain beyond the city is bare of trees or scrubs or fields. It is incredibly flat, without even the undulatory interruptions of sand dunes. It comes to an abrupt end at the stark, wind-eroded faces of the mountains of the Kirthar range. These are the lands where Mir Chakar, chieftain of the Rind tribe, fought a thirty-year war with Nawab Gwaharam, sardar of the Lasharis, over a beautiful Ja'at woman called Gohar—a war in which all forty-four *bolaks* (sardari houses) of the Baluchis became involved.

The mountains are hard and awesome. The valleys between them are sheer gorges, at the bottom of which fat-tailed sheep feed on sparse shrubs. The long train is hauled up the steep sides by the efforts of two huge diesel locomotives, one in front and one in back. It is an alternating landscape of cliffs and arid valley floors. Fierce winds, caught between the mountains, whirl themselves pointlessly around and around against the craggy faces of the rocks. Sometimes the train is suspended above dramatic precipices, and sometimes it crawls along empty riverbeds. It winds up through the Bolan Pass and rattles into the mile-high city of Quetta.

Quetta is a large small town. It is eminently a city of the Raj. It was an important garrison station in the days of the British (since it lies between the Bolan Pass to the southeast and the Khojak Pass to the northwest) and still is. The roads are broad and well laid-out and very clean, a rarity in much of Asia. The city seems to be run with a rigid efficiency whose standards have been set by its military origins. But Quetta has its own beauty: fruit trees in every private garden, quiet poplar-shaded avenues. The overall impression, however, is one of restraint rather than exuberance, order rather than lushness. Quetta's name comes from *kote*, which is Pashto for "fort." When Ahmed Shah Abdali, the conqueror who founded modern Afghanistan, came to India in 1759, he passed through the Khojak and Bolan passes before he crossed half the subcontinent to fight the Marathas outside Delhi. For services rendered, he awarded lands around Quetta to Mir Naseer, the Baluchi chieftain whose descendants are known as the khans of Kalat. The British secured Quetta from the khan of Kalat against a lease.

Modern Quetta was virtually rebuilt after the dreadful midnight earthquake of 1931 in which nearly half the city was shaken to rubble or fell into the steam-spouting chasms that opened in the ground. This rebuilding is one of the reasons the colonial flavor is more marked here than in any other Pakistani city. Today it is not only a garrison town and a provincial capital, it is a hill resort as well; and fashionable people from Karachi and other cities parade its streets when the summer makes the plains unbearable. Quetta is also the melting pot of the multi-ethnic province of Baluchistan, for it straddles the ethnic dividing line between the Pathan and Baluchi regions of the province. The vast, sparsely peopled territories of the Brahuis end nearby, in the south, and the tribal grounds of the Hazaras lie to the west. The streets of Quetta are thronged with people in many different costumes, and echo to the sound of a variety of languages and dialects.

But the bearded, turbaned Baluchi tribesmen and the tall, bronze Pathans and others seem uncomfortable and out of place in these quiet, colonial streets. They seem to be here only for one or the other incomprehensible bit of business, before returning to their hills and leaving the city to the government officials, soldiers, and vacationers. For Quetta is not the real Baluchistan. Urban society is far removed from the postures and sentiments of tribal reality. The real Baluchistan is found among the near-nomads, who wander in endless cycles over their tribal grounds and are administered by a proud sardar from his high-walled, fortified stone haveli. Or it is found among the quarreling farmers of the Pat area, or the fruit growers of Ziarat. Or it is seen on the long line of wave-cut cliffs and golden beaches from which the Makrani and Jamote fishermen set sail. These are the true Baluchistan—the Baluchistan that, like all things, is the product of its own past. The Baluchistan of the future is perhaps found in the strip-mined hills of Kalat and Lasbela, or in the awesome sprawl of the gas fields at Sui.

The Baluchi tribal system is very different from the Pathan. It was based not on communal property and an elected administrator-chieftain, but on the total authority of hereditary sardars. The law of primogeniture has been conspicuous by its absence in most Islamic societies; it was also absent from many other Asian societies. The colonial experience was an instrument of radical change (whether for better or worse depends on one's viewpoint) in the native authority structures of such societies, for the Raj legislated such concepts as hereditary ownership and authority, and the natural supremacy of the eldest son.

Traditional Baluchi society was exceptional among the loose, relatively diffused authority patterns that were characteristic of this part of the world. The Baluchi sardari, as far back as anyone has been able to record, has always been a hereditary office and has passed from father to eldest son. The concomitant of this principle has been the growth of rigid social pyramids in each tribe. Younger brothers and cousins of the tribal sardar are themselves smaller sardars owing their allegiance to the tribal head. Through these lesser nobles, the dictates of the sardar of each tribe are carried out.

There are many Baluchi tribes, each with its own territories. The origin of the Jamotes, one of the larger tribes, is a little obscure. It is believed by some that they may not be organic descendants from a common group of ancestors (as most other Baluchi tribes are believed to be), but that they were a looser original formation. They may well have once constituted a "federation" of small tribes. Today they live on the arid Lasbela coast of Baluchistan and in the hills to the north of the coast. There are also large Jamote settlements in parts of Lower Sind. The head of the Jamote tribe is the *jam sahib* (lord) of Lasbela. In addition to the traditional pastoral occupation they share with other Baluchis, the Jamotes are fishermen.

The dry hills of Lasbela descend to a low plateau. The plateau ends sharply on the coast, cut away by the sea in a wall of high cliffs. On a small bay below the cliffs, on a sweeping width of golden beach, is the Jamote fishing village of Gadani. The houses run down to the sands, stopping just short of the waterline. They catch prawn here—the largest, whitest, most succulent prawn in the world. In the winter they fish for sting-ray (which is called *pichar*). The flesh is eaten, the poison made into pseudomedical preparations. The wealthiest men in the village are the merchants who buy up the catch and auction it to city dealers for freezing, canning, drying, or sale in the towns. It is sent from here all over Pakistan, or it is exported to the United States.

To the north of the village, a brown thorn hedge and a low line of planted shrubs front the sand dunes. There is one house that stands just outside the boundary hedge. It is empty, and the sand has blown in through the doors and windows, covering the floor in an even carpet and making small heaps in the corners. The timbers of the roof have sagged and the walls are out of plumb. No one has lived in it for five years. But the outside corners of the roof are decorated with small colored pennants, and fresh flowers are placed at the door every so often. In the tiny courtyard behind the house is an unassuming double grave, the grave of the fisherman Ghaus Bux and of the woman he loved and married.

Ghaus Bux belonged to a village some distance down the coast, where he was known as the best fisherman. He had his own boat, and his luck with the catch was proverbial. Ghaus Bux loved the sea. The swell of the waves and the salt-tanged wind, the long days and nights of solitude as his nets collected their squirming victims, the rise and fall of his boat—these were his world. But when he returned, his holds filled with white and silver catch, he would watch wives and children rushing up the beach to the other fishermen and feel the pangs of loneliness. Ghaus Bux lived alone. He had no wife. He could have taken his pick of the girls of the village, but none of them attracted him.

One day out at sea, the wind was very strong. Gusts from an approaching storm tore one of Ghaus Bux's sails. He could not risk returning to his village in the storm, so he put into an unfamiliar bay for emergency repairs. As he worked on the beach, watching the heavy clouds on the horizon, he heard a voice singing. It was a woman's voice, but very strong and unutterably moving; the song was a Brahui ballad. Ghaus Bux left his work and went among the rocks to search for the singer. But the rocks were complex and deceptive, and he could not make out the direction of the voice. As he searched, the storm broke; the song stopped, and Ghaus Bux took shelter. He returned to his village, and over the next few weeks his colleagues were surprised at the meager catches their former champion brought back. Ghaus Bux's mind was not on fish; he spent his time at sea searching for the cove where he had heard the voice. But the Baluchistan coast is rocky, and there were few identifiable landmarks, even to his expert eye.

Soon it was time for the annual *mela* (fair). Ghaus Bux dressed in his finery—long shirt and pantaloons, a high-collared waistcoat and an elaborate turban—and set off with his friends. The mela was a riot of colors, sounds, and odors. There were tea stalls, food stalls, and games. There were stalls selling seashells and rare pebbles and fossils; there was jewelry made from shells and beads and onyx and silver; there were clothes and household goods and merchandise from the city. There was the hustle of people and the cries of hawkers and children and the din of recorded pop music. There were swings, and a small wooden Ferris wheel and whirling platforms for children. The place was thronged with people from all over the region. Ghaus Bux was dragged by his friends to participate in a tug-of-war, his village on one side of the thick rope and the nearby village of Gadani on the other. As he heaved and strained, his heels dug into the ground at the end of the line, Ghaus Bux heard a voice singing.

He released the rope, and his friends and the men from Gadani all fell in a sudden, protesting heap. Ghaus Bux ran toward the sound. He found a Brahui girl sitting in a circle of admiring people. "Who is she?" he asked. "She is the adopted daughter of the fisherman Majid Khan of Gadani village," he was told. "When she was little, she had a terrible fever and her tribesmen did not think she would live. Winter was coming, and they had to move on. Majid Khan offered to adopt her and nurse her back to health. He brought her from Kalat to Gadani, and here she is." Ghaus Bux was in love. He journeyed to Gadani and tried to persuade Majid Khan to give her hand in marriage. But the elderly fisherman did not approve of the match, for a reason best known to him. Ghaus Bux contrived to meet the girl on several occasions. Their courtship was arduous and difficult, and punctuated by his attempts to abduct his beloved from the village that would not permit their marriage. Eventually the girl's entreaties prevailed, and her foster-father grudgingly permitted the match.

Ghaus Bux brought his bride back to his village, and they lived happily together for four years. But all her children were stillborn. The village people blamed this on the fact of her non-Jamote ancestry and said the intertribal match was cursed. After the third stillborn child, they sneered vocally. Stung to the quick, Ghaus Bux divorced his wife and sent her back to Gadani. Within a few months he had married again, this time a girl from his village. His former wife was married off to a nephew of Majid Khan's. But Ghaus Bux was not happy with his second wife. He missed his first wife, and finally decided that he wanted her back. One day he set off from his village and walked the fifteen or so miles to Gadani. When he spoke to her, the girl protested that she was married and must stay with her husband. He begged and pleaded with her, but she was adamant. Her husband returned and there was a fight, during which Ghaus Bux received a serious knife wound.

He strayed, bleeding and weak, into the barren hills and rocks of the Lasbela coast, where he was found by a wandering fakir who nursed Ghaus Bux in his little lean-to in the desert. He fed him and kept him alive through the ferocious fever that wracked the young man's body and clouded his mind with delirium. Many months later, a fakir was seen approaching Gadani. As the bearded, loin-clothed figure came nearer, he was recognized as Ghaus Bux. He stood at the entrance of the village and declaimed: "As alms are the right of the beggar, so his wife is the right of a man. I come to beg for my wife. Please give me my wife."

He was chased away, but he came back during the night. In the morning the villagers found him sitting cross-legged at the entrance. "I will not go," he stated, "I will die here if she does not come with me." Every day and every night Ghaus Bux the fakir sat at the entrance of the village and refused to move. He sat very still, occasionally calling his wife's name. She came a few times and begged him to go away, but he refused. Days became weeks and weeks, months, but still he sat there. The villagers believed this miraculous, since to their knowledge he had had nothing to eat or drink in all this time. One morning many months later, they found him no longer sitting up but lying back with his eyes closed. They approached his emaciated form to find that he was dead. It is believed that there was a look of joy on his face. He had been united with his beloved, for the previous night his former wife had died of a sudden fever.

Her grief-stricken second husband moved from the house so that the fakir could be buried with his wife. The house itself was separated from the village by rebuilding the boundary hedge. It stands now a half-mile from the beach where the men push their hand-made, hand-oiled boats out to sea on logs of wood placed one after the other. To the east of Gadani, the cliffs come down to the sea and culminate in a white limestone hill, grained with green marble and slowly melting away into the salt water. On the other side of the cliffs is a shipyard where businessmen from distant cities disassemble and turn to salvage the rusted derelicts of the sea. It is another of the many faces of the Indus Valley.

THE INDUS VALLEY TODAY

The Indus valley today is 60 million people. It is fifty-five centuries of history in a climate that alternately scorches and freezes. It is a river that never quite reaches the sea; and it is the varying tangs of many curries. The Indus Valley is a very old, very young country.

In a suburb of Karachi a student sits on a traffic island reading a book. It is midnight. His parents' home has no electricity, so he studies by street lamp. A passing water carrier offers him a draught from the cool goatskin slung across his shoulders.

In a village near Peshawar, a grizzled Pathan elder scoffs at news of the Apollo landing. "How can men be walking on the moon?" he asks, pointing upward. "Look at how small it is. They would just fall off it." A factory worker in Lahore says, "So the white men have reached the moon now. I suppose they'll soon have direct radio contact with God."

A group of girls bathes in a low canal. An unexpected stranger suddenly appears, and the water is too shallow to sink modestly into. It is their faces they cover with their hands, and not their glistening bodies. The canals in the north are chocolate brown with the silt they carry. In the south they are a startlingly clear green.

In a film studio in Karachi, a group of tinsel-clad girls is dancing in front of the cameras. Their bare calves and arms weave in a popularized depiction of a country dance. The film studios of Lahore and Karachi manufacture as many films a year as Hollywood.

A young Baluchi housewife sits at the door of her mud and thatch cottage. She is weaving rush curtains to hang in the windows. She will sprinkle them with water and they will turn the furnace breath of the desert wind to fragrant coolness as it enters her home.

A business executive in Karachi argues with his boss over the provision of a car allowance in his salary. There are more automobiles in Cleveland, Ohio, than in the whole of Pakistan.

Acknowledgments

A book as many-sided as this one can never be said to have a single author. It is the product of many years of observation of, and response to, a land and its people. It has evolved out of reading and experiences, out of conversations with scholars, political leaders, and personal friends. It is, in fact, a synthesis of all I have absorbed from any number of sources.

Compiling an adequate list of those to whom thanks are due is therefore a formidable task. There are, however, a few people without whose assistance and patience nothing would have been possible: Mr. Porter McCray of the John D. Rockefeller III Fund, New York; Miss Jeannine Ciliotta and Mr. Dana Levy of John Weatherhill, Inc., Tokyo; Mr. Omar Kureishi of Karachi; Mr. Azim Khan of Karachi; Mr. Iftikhar Rasool of Elite Publishers Limited, Karachi; Mr. S. H. Zaidi of Karachi; Syeda Abida Hussain of Lahore; and Mr. Richard Shepard of Denver, Colorado, whose advice and support kept typewriter and camera functioning simultaneously and effectively.

Salman Tarik Kureshi, some of whose poems appear in this book, also lives in Karachi. He describes himself as a "marketing executive, a newspaper columnist, and an occasional verse-maker." With two exceptions, the poems in this book were written specifically for the occasion at the request of the author.

To each of these individuals, and to all the Pakistanis whose lives enriched this book, my sincere thanks.

S. Q.

The "weathermark" identifies this book as having been planned, designed, and produced at the Tokyo offices of John Weatherhill, Inc. Book design and typography by Samina Quraeshi and Dana Levy. Text composed and printed by General Printing Company, Yokohama. Engraving and printing by Nissha Printing Company, Kyoto. Bound at Okamoto Binding Company, Tokyo. The type of the main text is set in 14-pt Monotype Bell with hand-set Bell for display.